URUGUAY

ABOUT THE BOOK AND AUTHOR

This concise introduction to Uruguay examines the country's social, economic, and political life to determine how a nation called the "Switzerland of Latin America" could fall into stagnation and dictatorship and then regain its constitutional democracy. Within a multidimensional framework, Dr. Weinstein analyzes the roots of Uruguay's sophisticated welfare state (Batllismo) and the collapse of the system into economic and political crisis in the 1960s and 1970s. The rise of the Tupamaro urban guerrillas, state terror, the role of political parties and political culture, and the nature of military rule from 1973 to 1984 are also given careful attention. The author concludes with an evaluation of the redemocratization process in Uruguay and the prospects for consolidating democracy while maintaining economic stability.

Martin Weinstein is professor and chair of the Department of Political Science at the William Paterson College of New Jersey and adjunct professor of politics in the graduate program in Latin American studies at New York University. He has written extensively on Uruguay and U.S.–Latin American relations, including *Uruguay: The Politics of Failure* (1975) and *Revolutionary Cuba in the World Arena* (1979).

URUGUAY

Democracy at the Crossroads

Martin Weinstein

Westview Press / Boulder and London

Westview Profiles/Nations of Contemporary Latin America

Tables 1.1 and 1.2 reprinted by permission of St. Martin's Press, Inc.; Table 1.3, copyright 1954, reprinted by permission of The Trustees of Rutgers College in New Jersey; Table 4.1 reprinted by permission of Latin American Program, the Wilson Center.

Published in 1988 in the United States of America by Westview Press, Inc.; Frederick A. Praeger, Publisher; 5500 Central Avenue, Boulder, Colorado 80301

Library of Congress Cataloging-in-Publication Data
Weinstein, Martin.
  Uruguay, democracy at the crossroads.
  (Nations of contemporary Latin America)
  Bibliography: p.
  Includes index.
  1. Uruguay—Politics and government—1904–1973.
2. Uruguay—Politics and government—1973–
3. Uruguay—Economic conditions—1918–
4. Military government—Uruguay—History—20th
century.   5. Uruguay—Social conditions.   I. Title.
II. Series: Westview profiles.   Nations of contemporary
Latin America.
F2728.W43   1988   989.5   87-10519
ISBN 0-86531-290-7

Printed and bound in the United States of America

The paper used in this publication meets the requirements of the American National Standard for Permanence of Paper for Printed Library Materials Z39.48-1984.

10   9   8   7   6   5   4   3   2   1

for my father,
Louis A. Weinstein

Contents

Illustrations

Foreword

Stable democracy has been very difficult to achieve in Latin America, where even in the post–World War II era the vast majority of countries have experienced several swings of the pendulum toward dictatorial rule. Two exceptions stand out, both small, homogeneous, essentially agrarian societies. One, Costa Rica, is situated in Central America; the other, Uruguay, is in the Southern Cone of South America. The former managed to sustain both democratic forms and substance through the violent and prolonged swing to modern military authoritarian regimes that characterized the politics of the region from the early 1960s through the mid-1970s. Uruguay, however, could not withstand the forces that propelled all but the northernmost tip of South America into dark and often disastrous years of suspension of democratic processes. Its structures and culture did, however, resist this trend long after its neighbors had succumbed to the forces unleashed by the "crisis of populism."

What really sets Uruguay apart is both the gradual, step-by-step manner in which this descent into dictatorship happened and the heavy influence that events in its large neighbors played in the demise of Uruguay's city-state brand of democracy. In sharp contrast to Costa Rica—situated between Nicaragua and Panama, both small, though strategic countries—Uruguay is a fragile buffer between the two major powers of the South American continent. One shoe dropped for Uruguay when the dynamics of the bureaucratic authoritarian regime in Brazil brought harder-line elements to power by the later 1960s; the other dropped with the accentuated belief by successive military governments in Argentina that liberal, civilian-run Uruguay provided too much of a safe haven for their domestic foes. Thus, the breakdown of democracy, initiated after the 1966 elections and picking up momentum during the Gestido, Bordaberry, and Pacheco Areco governments, took place in a country subjected to nearly irresistible pressures by neighbors with forty and ten times its population and resources.

Having devoted most of his academic career to the close study of Uruguay, Professor Weinstein is admirably qualified to analyze both the peculiar and delicate flower that was Uruguay, the early welfare state democracy, and the special nature of the authoritarian regime that came to span more than a decade of its recent history. Yet his contribution to the comparative study of Latin America goes well beyond this, as he painstakingly describes the transition back to a democratic system in the past few years and comprehensively lays out the problems facing Uruguayans today as they try to consolidate democracy in a country with limited natural resources and a very fragile economic structure.

Clearly, as *Nations of Contemporary Latin America* moves away from its early concentration upon Central America and the Caribbean into the Southern Hemisphere, Dr. Weinstein's comprehensive and insightful treatment of this relatively little studied case—one rich in potential for broadened comparative understanding of the processes at work in the area—is a most appropriate inaugural volume for the Southern Cone.

Ronald Schneider
Queens College, CUNY

Preface and Acknowledgments

Myths die hard. The image of Uruguay as the "Switzerland of South America"—or as the Uruguayans themselves used to say, "*Como el Uruguay no hay*" (there's no place like Uruguay)—was based on a reality that began to fade badly by the mid-1950s.

During the first half of this century, Uruguay's small, homogeneous, and highly urbanized population lived under the joint benefits of a livestock economy tied to the British market and the sophisticated political institutions and welfare policies promoted by José Batlle y Ordóñez in the period prior to the Great Depression. The Batllista legacy was so powerful that Batlle's party, the Colorados, controlled the executive branch of government from 1903 until the 1958 elections, and even the Blanco governments from 1959 to 1967 were locked into the model. The system gave the average Uruguayan a middle-class life-style and access to an excellent education and health-care infrastructure. The seemingly endless bounty made possible an extraordinarily democratic and complicated electoral system that prided itself on the ability of almost any group or faction to receive voice and representation, especially if it belonged to one of the two traditional parties. In sum, the Uruguayan system of the 1940s and 1950s was civil, participatory, distributive, and stable.

What was to change all this? The short answer is economic decline signaled by the flagging of the populist experiment based on import-substitution economic growth and the failure of political elites to change policies and programs in the face of changing domestic and international realities.

Uruguay lost its civility along with its economic well-being by the late 1960s, a decade in which its growth rate was the worst in the hemisphere with the exception of Haiti—no great accomplishment. Political sectarianism, which had been masked by a homogeneous middle-class population's infatuation with the game of politics, became ugly as the economy worsened. Institutions that had managed to contain conflict in the past proved to be inadequate. The collegial executive was replaced in the 1967 constitution by a more powerful single executive. Unrest increased in the university and secondary schools. The trade union movement was radicalized. The Left began to unify in opposition to the Blanco and Colorado hold on the electorate. The Tupamaro guerrilla movement emerged out of frustration and idealism. And, most important, most Uruguayans clung to a security blanket of welfare-state populism that was dying with hardly anyone really noticing. The military would quickly wake everyone up with a nightmare that was all too real.

I dealt with some of these themes and issues in 1975 in my first book, *Uruguay: The Politics of Failure*. This volume will not ignore the historical context, and it will build on the knowledge and controversy engendered by its predecessor. I hope this work will give the reader an understanding of how Uruguay developed and how it misdeveloped. But the bulk of this study will concentrate on the decline of Uruguay's "exceptionalism," the nature and effects of the twelve-year military dictatorship, and the exciting, if problematic, reconstruction of democracy that Uruguay has undergone in the last two and one-half years, as was revealed to me during three trips I made to Montevideo during that time.

This work would not have been possible without the courage of the Uruguayan people and the support of my friends and colleagues, most especially, Louise Popkin, Ronald Hellman, Juan Rial, and Freida Silvert. As always, I owe my greatest debt of gratitude to my wife, Ruth, without whose inspiration and encouragement this book would not have come to be.

Martin Weinstein

1

The Land and the People: A Heritage of Moderation and Culture

The Oriental Republic of Uruguay sits between Argentina and southern Brazil at the beginning of the remarkable estuary known as the Río de la Plata (see Map 1.1). The nation's official designation as the Oriental Republic stems from its location on the east bank of the Río Uruguay; that river, the border between Argentina and Uruguay, flows into the River Plate estuary. Prior to independence in 1828, the country was known as the Banda Oriental (eastern shore).

THE LAND

Uruguay is the smallest country in South America; its land area of approximately 72,000 square miles is about the size of North Dakota. Even so, its territory is equal to that of Nicaragua, El Salvador, and Costa Rica combined. Uruguay has no significant mountain ranges, its highest peak being only 1,644 feet high. Its undulating grasslands contain no significant mineral resources, but almost 90 percent of its land surface is capable of growing crops, and 70 percent is tillable soil. The country shares the flatness of the Argentine pampa but not the richness of soil with which its neighbor is blessed. In this regard it has much more in common with the land of southern Brazil, Río Grande do Sul, of which, in fact, it is a natural extension.

Uruguay is almost totally bordered by water. Only some 175 miles of its 1,147 miles of geographical boundaries are not ocean, river, or estuary. Sitting in the La Plata basin, which is fed by the Parana and Uruguay rivers, the country has excellent hydroelectric resources. In addition to the Río Uruguay, the country's other major river is the Río

1

Map 1.1 Uruguay. Source: *Introduction to Uruguay* (Washington, D.C.: Pan American Union, n.d.), p. 1.

Negro, which begins in southern Brazil and continues for some 500 miles down the middle of Uruguay. On the eastern border of Uruguay is the Atlantic Ocean and toward its northeastern limit is a large tidal lagoon, Laguna Merin, that it shares with Brazil. The southern coast is bounded by the Río de la Plata estuary on which Montevideo, with its excellent harbor, is situated.

Uruguay's strategic location makes it a geographic—and thus political—buffer between Brazil and Argentina, and its viability has always been historically important to the commercial trade of the entire region. It was for this reason that the British became increasingly interested in the stability and independence of the Banda Oriental, a goal aided by rising political consciousness in the region that led, with British diplomatic intervention, to political sovereignty.

RACIAL AND ETHNIC COMPOSITION

Uruguay is a country of European stock. Some 90 percent of the population is of Spanish or Italian heritage. The small Indian population the Spanish encountered when they arrived in the seventeenth century was killed off, fled, or eventually intermarried, so that by the 1850s there were no pure-blooded Indians left. Two small Indian tribes in the Banda Oriental when the Spaniards arrived, the Charrúa and the Chana, had been pushed there by the expanding Guaraní empire in Paraguay. Indians resisted the first European explorers and in fact killed many members of the first expedition in 1516. The Indians' continued resistance slowed colonization in the area during the sixteenth and early part of the seventeenth century. Eventually they were displaced by the growing groups of Argentines and Brazilians who entered the Banda pursuing cattle and horses. It is estimated that the Mestizos (mixed Indian-Europeans) may comprise 5 to 8 percent of the total population, and they are concentrated in the northern provinces along the Brazilian border.

The black population numbers some 40,000–60,000. In the second half of the nineteenth century thousands of African slaves were brought to Montevideo. By the end of that century, blacks constituted 20 percent of the population of Montevideo and thus an important part of the labor force. With the influx of Europeans, the black population came to represent a smaller and smaller faction. Although some blacks still live in the area of Montevideo known as the Cerro, where some of the meat-packing plants are located, the majority of the black and mulatto population is found in the northern departments near the Brazilian border.

Uruguay's Jewish population has declined tremendously in the last two decades. Estimated at 40,000 in 1970, the community is now considered to number less than 25,000. Most of the Jews left because of the deteriorating economic situation and the rise of military dictatorship. Jews are active in the legal and medical professions and in some commercial enterprises. Originally attracted to Uruguay by its stable democratic and secular culture, they were never active in the political arena. Although living in Montevideo and involved in the liberal professions, they have been heavily Colorado in their political loyalties.

Uruguay's first census, taken in 1908, showed a total population of 1,042,686. Uruguay, like Argentina, had thus apparently experienced a huge growth in population during the preceding generation, owing to an influx of Spanish and Italian immigrants. The census indicated that an incredible 42 percent of the population of Montevideo was

TABLE 1.1
Estimated Total Population and Demographic Rates, 1895-1975
(five-year averages)

	Total population (thousands)	Births	Deaths	Natural increase	Migration	Total increase
			(rate per thousand)			
1895-99	826.3	43.4	14.8	28.6	0.1	28.7
1900-04	934.8	38.9	13.7	25.2	0.9	26.1
1905-09	1054.5	37.6	14.0	23.6	2.2	25.8
1910-14	1189.5	36.5	13.5	23.0	1.3	24.3
1915-19	1318.8	31.9	14.1	17.8	0.2	18.0
1920-24	1448.4	30.1	12.6	17.5	2.6	20.1
1925-29	1606.5	28.6	11.9	16.7	3.9	20.6
1930-34	1758.8	25.8	11.5	14.3	1.2	15.5
1935-39	1880.6	22.3	11.1	11.2	0.6	11.8
1940-44	1991.6	21.6	10.3	11.3	-0.1	11.2
1945-49	2111.5	21.1	9.1	12.0	0.5	12.5
1950-54	2263.4	21.2	8.5	12.7	1.4	14.1
1955-59	2436.4	21.8	8.8	13.0	.04	13.4
1960-64	2611.4	22.0	8.6	13.4	0.4	13.8
1969-71[a]	n.a.	22.1	9.6	12.5	n.a.	n.a.
1975[b]	2781.8	21.1	9.9	11.2	-5.4	5.8

[a]Three-year average
[b]1975 only
Source: M.H.J. Finch, A Political Economy of Uruguay Since 1870
(New York: St. Martin's Press, 1981), p. 24.

foreign born; the figure for the country as a whole was 17 percent. The data in Table 1.1 show that the growth in population, explosive around the turn of the century, has been meager in the last two decades.

According to the 1985 census, Uruguay has a population of just under 3 million inhabitants, up only slightly from the 2.6 million at the time of the 1963 census. The low birthrate and heavy emigration of the last two decades, both a reflection of economic decline and political breakdown, account for this very slow growth in population. By 1970 Uruguay had the lowest percentage of population under fourteen years of age and the highest percentage over sixty-five years of age of any country in Latin America. It is estimated that the median age in Uruguay, as of 1986, is 40, easily the highest in Latin America and one of the highest in the world.

Montevideo, because of its strategic location on the River Plate, has always been the principal city of Uruguay and, from the beginning of the country's history, has contained a significant percentage of its population. In recent decades, the economic stagnation of rural areas has led to an internal migration to Montevideo that has maintained the city's population even in the face of the significant (some might say extraordinary) emigration the country has experienced since the 1960s.

SOCIAL STRUCTURE

Uruguay, especially by Third World or Latin American standards, is a middle-class country. Whether we characterize the middle stratas by economic, social, educational, or valorative criteria, Uruguay, and especially the subsystem of Montevideo, may be characterized as middle class. As Antonio Grompone concludes in his study *Las Clases Medias en el Uruguay:* "Synthesizing, then, Uruguay is . . . a country in which members of the middle class, urban as well as rural, and those who have ties with governmental activities predominate in everything. This explains the idiosyncracies of their mentality and the social interest that appears in the resolution of particular types of conflicts—political, economic and social."[1]

The domination by the middle class of the political and economic life of the capital, coupled with the European ethnic profile, created a sense of a totally integrated society. Although this picture of social integration may be accurate within the capital, it does not accurately reflect the differences between urban and rural Uruguay. The split between city and countryside is wide and deep. Almost four-fifths of Uruguay's industrial production takes place in or around Montevideo. The census shows that there are four times as many people per physician in the interior as there are in the capital. Infant mortality is twice as high in the interior as it is in Montevideo, and a higher proportion of the population in rural areas is under fifteen years of age. More important, life chances in terms of schooling show a significant geographic variation. The proportion of students completing *liceo* (high school) and going on to the university drops precipitously as one moves away from Montevideo.

Uruguay can be accurately described as a city-state in spite of the fact that historically its export capability has been determined by its livestock and agricultural sectors. The 1985 census showed a total population of 2,921,000, of which Montevideo's population of 1,297,000 is an extraordinary 44 percent. To comprehend the overwhelming importance of Montevideo, it should be noted that Salto, the second largest city in Uruguay, has only 81,000 people and that there are only three other urban centers with more than 50,000. Montevideo's dominance is not simply based on population, however. Uruguay's public university (in 1985 a small private Catholic university was established, in Montevideo) is located in Montevideo, as are all of the country's major newspapers and television and radio stations. Over 70 percent of the country's industrial production is concentrated in the department of Montevideo. There is no residency requirement for election to the Senate

Young people in Montevideo. Photo courtesy of Dirección Nacional de Relaciones Públicas del Uruguay.

or Chamber of Deputies, and thus almost all of Uruguay's politicians live and work in Montevideo.

AGRICULTURE AND LIVESTOCK

The land has historically been the heart of Uruguay's economy. The soil is not particularly rich; however, it is suited to the natural grazing of the millions of cattle and sheep that are the mainstay of the country's exports. In 1985 this country of barely 3 million people contained over 9 million head of cattle and 23 million sheep. The extensive use of natural pastures has given Uruguay a land-use productivity figure of some 90 percent, but it is important to remember that most of this land is unimproved pasture. Nevertheless, the ranches, farms, and facilities for dairy production have many of the characteristics of the *minifundia* (small, subsistence farms) and *latifundia* (large farms) found elsewhere in Latin America (see Table 1.2).

Livestock were turned loose in the Banda Oriental by the Spanish under Hernando Arias in 1603. The wild herds multiplied so rapidly that by the time of the founding of Montevideo in 1726 there were an estimated 25 million head of cattle in the region. The result was the designation of the subsequent period in Uruguay as the "Age of Leather."

TABLE 1.2
Agrarian Structure and Performance: Distribution of Land
by Farm Size Categories, 1908-1970

	1908	1913	1937	1951	1956	1961	1966	1970
Percent distribution of farms								
Large	8.7	6.1	4.7	4.2	4.0	4.4	4.9	5.1
Medium	35.2	32.4	23.8	21.8	20.9	20.8	21.7	22.0
Small	56.1	61.5	71.5	74.0	75.1	74.8	73.4	72.9
Percent distribution of land								
Large	64.2	55.5	n.a.	56.5	55.8	56.9	58.4	58.4
Medium	30.8	35.7	n.a.	34.3	34.7	34.3	33.7	34.0
Small	5.0	8.8	n.a.	9.2	9.5	8.8	7.9	7.6

Source: M.H.J. Finch, A Political Economy of Uruguay Since 1870
(New York: St. Martin's Press, 1981), p. 105.

Cowhides were the product that would attract the gaucho to the Banda Oriental for the next 150 years. Only with the salting and curing of meat and the increased demand for tallow did the agricultural activity take on some diversification. The opening of a meat extract plant by Liebig at Fray Bentos in 1864 is viewed as the beginning of the modern meat industry in Uruguay. When the *saladeros*, or meat-salting plants, were replaced by the first refrigeration plants (*frigoríficos*), which prepared chilled, frozen, or canned beef, Uruguay's product was finally available to the European market. The introduction of refrigerated ships during the last two decades of the nineteenth century led to the rapid expansion of beef and lamb exports.

The Uruguayan grasslands that W. H. Hudson called the "Purple Land" in his remarkable semiautobiographical volume by that name enjoy a temperate climate broken only by some violent winter storms that are the result of the cold winds of Antarctica coming up against the subtropical air of southern Brazil. Uruguay has little forest (some 3 percent of its land surface) and no hydrocarbon resources. Its only mineral wealth consists of some semiprecious stones such as amethyst and topaz.

Uruguay's agricultural sector has historically been abundant and kind to the 3 million people it now serves, but stagnation and decline have left rural Uruguay relatively inefficient and unproductive in the face of changing international market conditions. The Uruguayan *campo* can be roughly divided into three distinct production areas. In the South, near the capital, the land is exploited intensively to provide Montevideo with fruits and vegetables. The North is the site of the extensive ranches

TABLE 1.3
Land Distribution in Uruguay in 1951

Size of holding (acres)	Number	Number as percent of total number of holdings	Area (acres)	Area as percent of total area
Under 12.5	10,953	13	71,939⎫	
12.5-25	11,117	13	189,350⎬	2
25-50	13,771	16	476,441⎭	
50-125	16,910	20	1,321,485	3
125-250	10,375	12	1,809,127	4
250-500	7,814	9	2,725,936	7
500-1,250	7,241	9	5,611,875	13
1,250-2,500	3,475	4	6,036,623	15
2,500-6,250	2,452	3	9,409,969	22
6,250-12,500	763⎫		6,381,672	15
12,500-25,000	316⎬	1	5,099,932	12
Over 25,000	71⎭		2,790,522	7
Totals	85,258	100	41,924,871	100

Source: Cited in Russell H. Fitzgibbon, Uruguay: Portrait of
a Democracy (New Brunswick, N.J.: Rutgers University Press, 1954),
p. 76.

on which sheep and cattle are raised. The eastern farm belt of the country serves as the principal grain- and cereal-producing region.

The principal livestock export products are wool and beef, although milk and cheese products are also produced in abundance. Corn is grown as a feed concentrate, wheat for bread, and rice both for domestic consumption and as an increasingly important export crop. Beet sugar accounts for 80 percent of sugar production, but total sugar production only accounts for 50 percent of the country's consumption.

Although one cannot speak of a famous "Fourteen Families" as in El Salvador, and the distribution of land has never been a pressing political issue (as Uruguay is underpopulated), concentration of ownership has always been a reality. The data in Table 1.3 describe land distribution in Uruguay in 1951, at the height of the country's economic well-being after World War II.

The 1980 census showed that 5.7 percent of farms controlled 56.6 percent of the land, whereas 68.6 percent of the farms or ranches comprised only 6.9 percent of the land. In addition, most of the large landholdings are of unimproved pastureland and employ very few ranch hands. The number of agricultural workers, which stood at 293,000 in 1956, is believed to number over 150,000 in 1987.

If we group the departments that are the sites of extensive livestock raising—Durazno, Rivera, Rocha, Tacuarembo, Cerro Largo, La Valleja, and Flores—we encounter an increasingly depopulated countryside with fewer and fewer salaried workers. The ranches in these areas are referred to as estancias cimarronas (wild ranches) because of the lack of productive activity.

The most productive rural area in Uruguay is in the Southeast—the departments of Río Negro, Soriano, and Colonia—where wheat, other cereals, milk, and cheese production make the area the country's breadbasket. The southernmost departments of San José, Canalones, Florida, and the agricultural area of Montevideo itself are devoted to the intensive production of the fruits, vegetables, and wine that provision the capital. Yet even this area lost 10,000 workers in the decade of the 1970s because of the reduced demand precipitated by economic decline and the collapse of the beet-sugar industry, which lost its subsidy in 1975.

The underclass in the countryside lives in shantytowns that are referred to as *rancheríos* or *poblaciones de ratas* (rat towns). Their numbers are dwindling but it is estimated that at least 300,000 people, or 10 percent of Uruguay's population, live in these communities.

Surprisingly, several departments have shown significant population growth. The northern province of Artigas experienced growth along the border with Brazil, most especially in the area around the town of Bella Union, with its agroindustrial cooperatives. The department of Treinta y Tres has attracted labor because of the successful growth of its rice-exporting industry. The department of Maldonado's growth was caused by its proximity to the resort community of Punta del Este and the construction boom there in 1979 and 1980.

In the past, Uruguay's economic health has been based on a dynamic export economy and the conscious distribution of its benefits. Uruguay was built on cattle and sheep, the products of which—wool, meat, and hides—were fortunately tied to the voracious appetite of a Britain propelled by the industrial revolution. This was especially true at the beginning of the twentieth century when, in the period dominated by José Batlle y Ordóñez (1903–1929), the value of exports doubled, principally because of the market for frozen meat. In 1930, just before the Great Depression, all chilled beef, 83 percent of mutton, and 39 percent of frozen beef went to Britain.

Uruguay's industry has been based on the processing of meat and wool and the production of domestic consumables, with the food and beverage industry making the largest contribution. Meat processing and dairy production are the most important activities, followed by textile manufacturing. These industries grew as a result of the urban welfare-oriented distributive policies of Batllismo (as the ideology and policies of José Batlle are known) but received an extra stimulus from the import-substitution industrialization policies that reached their peak in the late 1940s and early 1950s.

Uruguay's agricultural production is most notable for its slow growth throughout the century—despite the expansion of exports—and its

The economic basis of Uruguay's welfare state. Photo courtesy of Dirección Nacional de Relaciones Públicas del Uruguay.

stagnation since the early 1960s. Lack of investment is a crucial factor in this phenomenon, and it is in this regard that the policies of mostly urban-oriented Colorado governments should be examined. The usual denunciation of Colorado governments for killing the golden calf—that is, destroying the incentive for productive investment in the agricultural sector by promoting proindustrial welfare-state policies—finds its most famous expression in Julio Martínez Lamas' *Riqueza y Pobreza del Uruguay: Estudio de las Causas que Retardan el Progreso Nacional* (*Wealth and Poverty in Uruguay: A Study of the Causes That Retard National Progress*) published in 1930.[2] M.H.J. Finch, however, has demonstrated that José Batlle's fiscal policies, although clearly conscious of their redistributive activities, do not account for rural stagnation. Rather, Finch argues that the *latifundistas* themselves were not interested in investing in the intensification of land use, and that the outflow of capital from the rural sector was voluntary before 1930.

Batlle took advantage of the funds generated by the livestock sector and the rapid urbanization of Montevideo to build a political base that gave the Colorado party the power to expand the social welfare functions of the state, buy social peace, and strengthen political institutions. At the time he came to power, 30 percent of the country's population already lived in Montevideo. The most extraordinary legacy of Batllismo was the integration of this population into a stable two-party democratic political system.

EDUCATION

The transformation of public education in Uruguay was the crowning achievement of José Pedro Varela, a friend and disciple of Horace Mann. Varela served in the administration of Lorenzo Latorre (1876–1880), whose regime was the closest thing to an integrating dictatorship that Uruguay would experience in the nineteenth century. His work led in 1877 to the passage of the Law of Common Education, which established the principle of free, secular, and compulsory primary education. Central government expenditures on education during the twentieth century have been among the highest in Latin America. Even as late as 1968, during a very troubled time for Uruguay politically and economically, such expenditures were the second highest in Latin America.

There are several excellent private schools in Uruguay; the British School is considered the best and the one to which most of the elite send their children. Primary-school enrollment quadrupled from 1880 until the time of Batlle's death in 1929. From 1930 to 1963 the index of primary enrollment rose from 100 to 226. The numbers are equally impressive for secondary education. From 1950 to 1965 secondary-school enrollment was up 167 percent. In 1960 Uruguay had the highest percentage of secondary-school-aged population in school for all of Latin America. Education received enormous stimulus under José Batlle, to the extent that by 1930 over three-quarters of all children of primary-school age were attending school. By 1970 this figure was a remarkable 96 percent. Secondary-school enrollment increased some 600 percent between 1942 and 1970. These figures deteriorated somewhat under the

University of the Republic. Photo from U.S. Department of State, Bureau of Public Affairs, *Background Notes: Uruguay* (Washington, D.C.: U.S. Government Printing Office, 1985).

military dictatorship because of the economic difficulties encountered by the working class.

Uruguay's only public university is the University of the Republic located in Montevideo. It is divided into ten *facultades*, or schools, each of which has a high degree of autonomy through its dean and elected council. The university also has a specialized institute, the Instituto de Profesores Artigas, that turns out educational administrators and, more recently, is responsible for the training of career diplomats. Enrollment is open to everyone who successfully completes the secondary-school cycle, and tuition is free. In the past, the bulk of students enrolled in the schools of Medicine and Law. The majority of students are from the middle or upper class from Montevideo or from urban centers in the interior. Most students consider themselves to be liberal, and the Federation of University Students of Uruguay (FEUU, Federación de Estudiantes Universitarios del Uruguay) is dominated by leftist activists. As the system is modeled after those of continental Europe, most students' degree programs are five to six years in length. In practice, the typical student will spend at least two more years completing all his or her requirements. In 1964, when things were far more "normal" in the university than they have been since that time, one-quarter of all students had been in the university ten years or longer; during that time, enrollment was 15,000, but the average graduating class numbered only 750. The yearly number of graduates as a percentage of incoming students fell from an average of 56 percent in the 1940s to less than 30 percent in the late 1950s and early 1960s. The situation became even worse in the late 1960s and early 1970s because of student and political unrest.

These data are not totally indicative of the role of higher education in Uruguay. Of course, the university is supposed to provide for social mobility and the training of new professionals and the certification of elites. It performed these roles in the earlier part of the century and was a principal certifying mechanism for the sons and daughters of the middle class from the 1920s to the 1950s. However, a stagnant economy and the failure of political elites to get the country moving again took their toll on university productivity and the life chances of those who were graduated. It appears to me that, since the late 1960s, attending the university and thus being able to call oneself a *universitario* has become an occupational category for Uruguay's young adults. It is one way to keep the sons and daughters of the middle and upper stratas off the streets. Being a *universitario* may confer some status and a false sense of security, but it is not giving the society the scientifically and technologically trained cadres it will need for the twenty-first century. This is especially true because of the inadequate budgets for professors and equipment that has plagued the system for decades and continues to hamper it under President Julio María Sanguinetti's austerity budget.

The university population has expanded dramatically in the 1980s, from a total of 34,000 students in 1980 to over 78,000 in 1985. The number of new admissions skyrocketed in 1984 and 1985, undoubtedly reflecting the return to civilian government and optimism concerning the university. Law continues to be the most popular career option, with engineering enjoying increased student attention in recent years. It still takes over eight years for the average student to complete his or her degree.

ART AND CULTURE

For a small country with no great indigenous heritage, Uruguay's cultural life has been rich, varied, and influential. An early commitment to public education and cultural freedom contributed to this heritage, as did the European influence on artists and intellectuals.

Literary history and criticism have a strong tradition in Uruguay. A massive seventeen-volume study, *Historia Crítica de la Literatura Uruguaya*, was published in 1913 by Carlos Roxlo. Alberto Zum Felde's *Proceso Intelectual del Uruguay*, which appeared in 1930, remains the seminal work on Uruguay's intellectual and literary work during its first century of independence. The most enduring modern testament to artistic, intellectual, and literary criticism was *Marcha*, an independent weekly founded by Carlos Quijano in 1939. Until its closure by the dictatorship in 1974, *Marcha* was the proving ground for such brilliant writers and critics as Emir Rodríguez Monegal, Angel Rama, and Eduardo Galeano. There has never been a more erudite weekly on literature and politics in Latin America than *Marcha*, and its existence in Uruguay is a testament to the truth that cultural expression is not a function of size.

Uruguay's first writer of note was Juan Zorrilla de San Martín (1888–1931), a romantic novelist who infused his work with a spirit of nationalism. His most famous work is an epic poem, "Tabaré," recounting the history of Uruguay's small indigenous Indian tribe, the Charrúas. He also wrote a prose piece entitled "La Epopeya de Artigas," which exalted the virtues of the man considered to be the father of Uruguay's independence, José Gervasio Artigas.

The most famous Uruguayan man of letters is undoubtedly José Enrique Rodó (1872–1917), whose short masterpiece *Ariel*, written in 1900, remains the classic statement on the confrontation between South American spirit and culture and the materialism and drive for power that, for Rodó, characterized North American civilization.

Of Uruguay's major poets, Juana de Ibarbourou stands out among several accomplished female poets. Short stories are very popular among Uruguay's print-oriented population; Mario Benedetti and Juan Carlos Onetti are recognized as the most accomplished story writers; Benedetti's *Gracias por el fuego* (Thanks for the Fire) is considered the best novella written in Uruguay since the end of World War II.

The theater has always been popular in the Río de la Plata, and the most famous Uruguayan dramatist, Florencio Sanchez, is recognized as the country's greatest playwright, having brought social realism to the theater in the 1920s. In the contemporary period, Mauricio Rosencof, with such works as "Las Ranas," had already established himself as a popular playwright in the early 1960s, but gave up his literary career to help found the Tupamaro guerrilla movement. He has thus emerged as a controversial, if not notorious, figure. Since his release from prison in March 1985, many of his poems and plays, written in prison to help him survive the ordeal of torture and isolation to which he was subjected, have been published and performed to generally favorable critical review.

Uruguay's three most important artists are Juan Manuel Blanes, known for his lifelike historical scenes, Torres Garcia, and Pedro Figari. Figari's impressionistic scenes of rural life and folk dancing have gradually caused him to be recognized as one of South America's most important twentieth-century artists. A very important exhibition of his work took place at the gallery of the Center for Inter-American Relations in New York during 1985 and 1986.

Many newspapers are available in Uruguay, although far fewer than in the 1960s. None are very good. All the daily newspapers are identified with factions of the political parties, and journalistic standards are very low. The best newspaper currently published is a weekly independent publication, *Búsqueda*, which attempts fairly successfully to summarize the previous week's news and has extensive coverage of the economic situation. *Marcha* has been resurrected as *Brecha*, which despite some lively writing and commentary has not yet approached the level of its predecessor.

Regarding folk music, the gaucho gave Uruguay its national folk dance, the *pericón*, and the tango is almost as popular in Uruguay as it has been in Argentina. As for artisan crafts, a carved gourd known as a *maté* in which the tealike herb *maté* is brewed and carried is the most distinctive example of gaucho culture that has become a permanent fixture in everyday Montevideo. In more recent years, a cottage industry involving the hand-knitting of sweaters—Manos del Uruguay (Hands of Uruguay)—has proven very successful, with major exports to Europe and the United States.

As is clear from this brief discussion, for a small country, Uruguay has a rich and varied cultural and literary heritage. This heritage was nurtured by a sophisticated and democratic political and social system, the foundations of which are the subject of the following chapter.

2

The Historical Background

Juan Diáz de Solís, in 1516, was the first European to set foot on what was to become Uruguay. When he sailed into the great estuary that would come to be known as the Río de la Plata, thinking he had found the southern tip of South America, he and a shore party landed some 70 miles east of the current site of Montevideo. They were immediately killed by the Charrúas, a band of Indians who inhabited the region. This inhospitable beginning was followed by a frustrating search for mineral riches such as the conquistadores had found in Mexico and Peru. The muddy estuary was most likely given the name Silver River in the hope that it would lead its explorers to newfound wealth. As such hopes faded, the area on the right bank of the river—the Río Uruguay—that separates northeast Argentina from Uruguay came to be known as the Banda Oriental. It remained a virtually uninhabited territory until the cattle and horses that had been placed there in 1603 by Hernando Arias, the first locally born (*criollo*) governor of the area, had multiplied to the point that their hides became commercially profitable for some Buenos Aires ranchers and the cowboys known as gauchos.

There were no permanent settlements in Uruguay during the seventeenth century except for some camps set up on the Uruguayan side of the river to exploit the trade in hides. In 1680 the Portuguese moving south from Brazil founded an encampment at Colonia, directly across the river (some 25 miles wide at this point) from Buenos Aires. Thus began a rivalry that would help shape Uruguay's independence some 150 years later. Spaniards founded Montevideo farther east in 1726.

The modern history of Uruguay begins at the turn of the seventeenth century, when a series of British expeditions to the region showed that Spain was no longer able to effectively defend its possessions there and that trade with Britain offered new possibilities for profit. The desire by Buenos Aires to keep the Portuguese empire from expanding to the

16

The Uruguayan flag flying at the entrance to the Fort-Museum of San Miguel. Photo courtesy of National Office for Public Relations of the Oriental Republic of Uruguay.

Río de la Plata and the British desire to protect its newfound trade with the region would aid and abet Uruguayan nationhood.

THE ROOTS OF NATIONHOOD

José Gervasio Artigas (1764–1850) is the father of Uruguayan nationhood, its "George Washington," although he failed to establish his vision of a confederation of the provinces of the Río de la Plata, which would have included an independent Banda Oriental. General Artigas was a gauchoesque caudillo who, at the outbreak of the War for Independence in Buenos Aires in 1810–1811, found himself caught between three forces: a Spanish loyalist garrison in Montevideo, an independent junta in Buenos Aires that saw itself as the heir to a centralized vice-royalty of the Río de la Plata, and a Brazilian army with its own eye on the Banda Oriental. The on-again, off-again war between Buenos Aires and the Spaniards in Montevideo saw Artigas and his gaucho army trek hundreds of miles in a dogged attempt to maintain their autonomy and thus secure an independent future for Uruguay.

In April 1813, Artigas issued a written set of instructions to the Uruguayan delegates to a regional political conference in Buenos Aires. These "Instrucciones del Año XIII" embodied the principles of independence, republicanism, and confederation in which Artigas fervently believed.

From his base on the Río Uruguay, Artigas continued to press for a confederation of those provinces that bordered on the Río de la Plata. His efforts earned him the title of "Protector of Free Peoples." When Brazil once again invaded Uruguay in 1816, Artigas resisted not only the invaders, but his old centralist enemies in Buenos Aires. Forced into exile in Paraguay in 1820, he never returned, although he lived to see the creation of an independent Uruguay in 1828. He died a revered old warrior in 1850. Artigas is exalted irrespective of his checkered success; the Left and the Right equally invoke him to fulfill their own historical mythology.

The Banda Oriental was officially annexed by Brazil in 1820 and given the name of Cisplatine Province. In April 1825, thirty-three Uruguayan exiles, led by Juan Antonio Lavalleja, crossed the river from Buenos Aires to free their homeland from Brazil. The "Immortal Thirty-Three," as they would be known, ignited a rebellion that was quickly aided by Buenos Aires, which once again expected a freed Banda Oriental to become a province under the rule of the Argentine capital. The British, whose increasingly lucrative trade with the ports of the region was severely hampered by renewed hostilities between Brazil and Buenos Aires, now stepped in. England, through its diplomatic emissary, Lord Ponsonby, mediated the dispute, and in 1828 a treaty was signed between Brazil and Argentina that created the independent buffer state of some 80,000 citizens, officially known as the República Oriental del Uruguay.

Uruguay adopted its first constitution in 1830. The next seventy years were a period of great turmoil abetted by the continuing desire of Buenos Aires to have a subservient government in Montevideo. General José Fructoso Rivera, first president of Uruguay, deposed his successor, General Manuel Oribe, in 1838. Oribe, with help from Buenos Aires, laid siege to Montevideo for over a decade (the so-called Guerra Grande), during which time the city was defended with the aid of its French and Italian communities; among the Italians was Giuseppe Garibaldi, his country's future national hero. The siege of Montevideo was lifted in 1851. The rest of the century remained politically chaotic. As Simon G. Hanson described Uruguay's first seven decades of independence, "Of the twenty-five governments that guided the Uruguayan ship of state from 1830 to 1903, nine were forced out of power, two were liquidated by assassination, and one by grave injury, ten resisted successfully one or more revolutions, and three were free of serious disturbances during their period in office."[1]

The sophisticated two-party system that would become one of the dominant features of Uruguayan political life in the twentieth century began as little more than warring bands of gauchos. In 1836, at the Battle of Carpintería, General Oribe led those with federalist sympathies against General Rivera's more liberal urban elements. The factions distinguished themselves by wearing colored hatbands, white (*blanco*) for Oribe's forces and red (*colorado*) for Rivera's faction. Thus were born the Blanco (later also officially known as the Partido Nacional) and Colorado parties of Uruguay.

THE POLITICS OF COPARTICIPATION

As has just been shown, Uruguay's two traditional parties trace their origins to the civil wars between liberals and conservatives that Uruguay, like much of Latin America, experienced shortly after independence. The long and debilitating siege of Montevideo and the Guerra Grande (1838–1851) witnessed the establishment of Blanco-dominated government outside of Montevideo and a Colorado government in the capital. Out of this struggle emerged the identities of the two parties.

Pacts between the political parties would become a constant feature of Uruguayan history. The Paz de Abril in 1872 put an end to the uprising of Blanco caudillo Timoteo Aparicio and allowed the Blancos control of four of the thirteen departments into which the country was then divided. The more serious rebellion of Aparicio Saravia in 1897 ended with the Pacto de la Cruz, which gave the Blancos control of six of eighteen departments in the country—the peace agreement going so far as to state that if a citizen of one party moved out of a department that had been granted to the opposite party, he or she would be indemnified for such a move. This is but one example of the fierce party loyalty that weakened national unity and citizen loyalty to the state. Geographic control was important to the Blancos, for it would translate into Senate and Chamber of Deputy seats in national government. The Pacto de la Cruz was the first in a long series of party ageements that would attempt to guarantee political stability even as it produced, on occasion, significant political and social change.

By the end of the nineteenth century, Uruguay began to develop an institutionalized political mechanism that proved to be eminently successful for the containment of political conflict. Described as *coparticipación* (coparticipation) by its earliest practitioners, the term quickly became widely accepted to describe the peaceful sharing of formal political and informal bureaucratic power in Uruguay. In a narrow usage, it refers to the presence of members of the opposition party in government posts or on the directorship of state corporations. In a wider sense, it refers to the legitimation of the notion that the two traditional parties and their adherents had an inherent right to divide and share the process and product of government and governmental activities.

The uneasy truce between the Blancos and Colorados would explode for one final time in 1903 with the election of the brilliant Colorado leader, José Batlle y Ordóñez. Batlle's vision of a strong central government and a united country did not sit well with some of the rural Blanco leaders. Civil war erupted. Victory for the Colorados—and hence for the central government—was to end armed civil strife for six decades. Batlle consolidated his rule and produced the legacy of his welfare state.

Batlle served two terms as president (1903–1907, 1911–1915), separated by a term as president by his political protégé, Claudio Williman (1907–1911). The presidency became a powerful institution under Batlle, with Blanco participation at the national level aided by legislation that granted limited proportional representation in parliament. The political maneuvering over electoral legislation led to the passage in 1907 of the so-called "double simultaneous ballot," which would influence Uruguayan politics until the present. Under the provisions of this and subsequent legislation, separate factions (sublemas) of each party could run their own list of candidates for political office. These separate lists would be added together to determine the party's total vote. Essentially, then, a simultaneous primary and election is carried out by the voters. Obviously, this legislation allowed significant splintering of the traditional parties without damaging their overall performance. When this legislation was extended to include presidential elections in 1920, it further exacerbated the difficulties of maintaining coherent party politics.

Coparticipation took on renewed life as a result of Batlle's political bombshell—his call in 1913 for the creation of a collegial executive to be known as the Colegiado. Batlle's plan called for a nine-member Junta de Gobierno to be first elected on a winner-take-all basis and then renewed at the rate of one member a year. The Blancos opposed the proposal, seeing it as motivated by Batlle's desire to perpetuate his control of executive authority, but the project ran into unexpectedly severe opposition within the Colorado party itself.

Batlle's constitutional reform project and the cautious position of Batlle's successor, President Feliciano Viera, produced a serious split in the Colorado party that left the Batllistas as a faction, albeit the dominant faction of the party. In order to get some form of collegial executive system, Batlle was forced into a series of political compromises.

Batlle sincerely admired the Swiss collegial executive system. He also undoubtedly saw the project as a way to protect his programs against the day in 1915 when he would retire and could no longer succeed himself. Opposition to Batlle's reform was so intense that an election for a constitutional convention did not take place until 1916, and that election produced a victory for anti-Colegiado forces. Working behind the scenes, however, Batlle hammered out a deal with the Herrerista faction of the Blancos led by Luis Alberto de Herrera in June 1917, which led to a new constitution that took effect two years later. Reflecting a spirit of compromise, a bicephalous executive was created that consisted of a president whose functions included foreign affairs, national security, and internal order and a Consejo Nacional de Administración (National Council of Administration), which was in charge of all other executive government functions. The Consejo consisted of nine members, six from the majority party and three from the minority. The Blancos supported the project in return for electoral reforms guaranteeing the secret ballot and proportional representation.

In general, the Blancos agreed to the new constitution because they felt it gave them electoral guarantees and insured representation (coparticipation) in the executive branch. Blanco leader Martín Martínez argued in support of the new constitution that the new organ of executive authority gave his party something it had always lacked—interdictive power at the executive level. He hoped this power would be used to create a truly nonpoliticized bureaucracy, but, unfortunately, this hope would be dashed on the rocks of political reality.

Thus a Colegiado was established, but the office of president still survived. The National Council of Administration would oversee the day-to-day operations of government, whereas the president was responsible for security and foreign affairs. The 1920s were a period of marked equilibrium between the two traditional parties. The elections of the National Council of Administration were usually quite close; in 1925, Blanco leader Luis Alberto de Herrera became head of this body. The following year, however, he lost the national presidential election by only 1,500 votes. The parties' virtual parity in voting strength in the 1920s turned government policy into a series of compromises and close votes with little extension of the Batllista reforms. The system was actually quite inefficient, but booming exports and the distributive policies implemented through the previously erected Batllista institutions served the country well—at least until 1929 when Batlle died and the Great Depression began. The experiment in political compromise during the first Colegiado (1919–1933) culminated in the early 1930s in Blanco acquiescence to a policy of expansion of state economic activities; this was in exchange for an increased share of the patronage resulting from such expansion.

In this century, there was one period of extraconstitutional rule in Uruguay prior to the 1973 coup. It was precipitated by the economic crisis produced by the world depression in the 1930s and the rivalries within both the Colorado and Blanco parties following the death of José Batlle in 1929. President Gabriel Terra, on March 31, 1933, dissolved parliament and ruled dictatorially with the support of the Blanco faction led by Luis Alberto de Herrera. Only one person died in this coup; former president Baltasar Brum committed suicide while resisting the takeover. In 1934, Terra asked for and won approval of a new constitution that did away with the National Council ofAdministration (thus returning Uruguay to a purely presidential executive system) and creating a Senate whose membership was limited exclusively to the dominant factions of the two traditional parties—that is, those headed by Terra and Herrera. Elections took place in 1938 and resulted in an overwhelming victory for the Colorado candidate, Alfredo Baldomir. Blanco resistance to the government's tilt toward the Allied cause in 1941, and the improvement in Uruguay's economic fortunes, led to the normalization of government through a "coup" in 1942 that resulted in another constitutional reform eliminating the Terra-Herrera division of the Senate.

It is important to remember that the period from 1933 to 1942 was not one of military dictatorship. Some heavy-handed politicians reacting to an economic crisis and driven by personal vendetta and ambition altered the constitutional game. But there was no torture, no murder, no political prisoners, and little censorship. The military did not rule and, in fact, were never part of the decision-making process during this period. The return to full constitutional government was peacefully accomplished by a civilian elite and brought back with it was the full panoply of civil liberties and welfare-state practices that Uruguay had enjoyed for the first two-thirds of this century. The favorably economic climate created first by World War II and then by the Korean War, coupled with the emergence of new political leaders, especially in the Colorado party, quickly reaffirmed Uruguay's claim to its unique position as an island of democracy and stability in Latin America. This was the legacy of José Batlle, and it is to this theme that we now turn.

3

The "Switzerland of South America": The Batllista Legacy

Ideology matters—at least it seems that way to this observer. José Batlle y Ordóñez had an ideology and developed a program that combined have come to be known as Batllismo. Batlle's vision of a democratic, welfare-oriented polity would come to dominate Uruguayan politics for the first three decades of the twentieth century and would turn Uruguay into one of the most important political laboratories in Latin America.

Batlle's political genius rested on his recognition of the importance of the new immigrants and their children as an urban mass that could be made the backbone of the electoral strength of the Colorado party. He was particularly interested in attracting the loyalty of Montevideo's rapidly expanding labor force. By the turn of the century, Batlle threw the weight of his newspaper, *El Día*, behind the emerging union movement. After his electoral victory and the destruction of the Blanco opposition in the 1903–1904 civil war, Batlle began to flesh out his vision of an activist state that would promote the social and economic welfare of its citizens. At times Batlle would sound like a Marxist (which he certainly was not), but national politics and the attacks of political enemies both inside and outside the party caused him to temper his remarks and postpone much of his legislative agenda until his second term as president.

For Batlle, the task of an interventionist state was to bring about social justice. Such a state might act through legislation or by means of a greatly enhanced direct entrepreneurial role through which it would provide essential services or own and operate key commercial or industrial sectors—frequently as a public monopoly. The state institutions, most

José Batlle y Ordóñez. Photo courtesy of Ministerio de Instrucción Pública del Uruguay.

especially the state enterprises (or *entes autónomos*, as they are known in Uruguay), were designed to enhance the general welfare and ensure the international sovereignty of the country. They would prove to be Batlle's enduring legacy. State activities in hitherto private realms such as insurance, utilities, and mortgage banking would, according to Batlle's vision, serve the national interest by reducing the country's reliance on foreign expertise and capital.

The *entes autónomos* were a central bone of contention during the debates concerning the 1917 constitution. The issue was not necessarily their legitimacy—which was less questioned than it had been previously—but the question of their decentralization and autonomy from the central government. This was a sensitive issue for the Blancos, who had a justifiable right to fear that they would be denied access to jobs, that these *entes* would be turned into patronage machines for the governing Colorados. As we shall see, this issue would color the politics of administrative reform and the role of the state for decades to come and would be the influential determinant of constitutional reform. Nevertheless, the *entes* functioned, at least in their early years, as efficient engines of development and social change. For example, when the production of electricity was nationalized in 1911, output was 16 million kilowatts. By 1924 the total had expanded to 72 million. State enterprises were crucial to Uruguay's expansion during this period, even in the face of conservative resistance to Batlle's program.

To his critics' complaint that little Uruguay was not the proper venue for bold social and political experiment, Batlle had a quick reply, "We may be a poor and obscure mini-republic, but we will have advanced mini-laws."[1] Batlle wasn't about to stop at legislation that created an urban minimum wage, social security legislation, a state insurance and mortgage bank, and educational reforms. He saw the state as an economic organization that should "enter industry when competition is not practicable, when control by private interests vests in them authority inconsistent with the welfare state, when a fiscal monopoly may serve as a great source of income to meet urgent tax problems, when the continued export of national wealth is considered undesirable. State socialism makes it possible to use for the general good that portion of the results of labor which is not paid to labor."[2]

True to this vision, Batlle had the 1922 party convention call for profitsharing plans in state enterprises, inexpensive medical services, and increased taxes on land and inheritances. None of these proposals were implemented, especially those that would have touched the interests of large landowners. Batlle's rhetoric with regard to real property may have been radical, but political reality produced little change in agrarian structures or fiscal polity. The inability of Batllismo to carry out effective

land reform or implement its fiscal plans in regard to agriculture is seen
by most commentators as the Achilles heel of Batllismo, for as almost
all of them argue, Batlle's urban-oriented welfare state was erected on
the shifting fortunes of an untouched, increasingly unproductive, and
eventually noncompetitive export sector.

However, lack of success in this area must be understood in the
context of the times. In the first place, the mere threat of the measures
proposed by Batlle enabled the government to accomplish a massive
redistribution of income from the rural to urban sector and carry out
much of its social programs with resources derived from exports. Second,
splits in the Colorado party, which had been growing since the conflict
over the Colegiado, deprived Batlle of the internal unity that would have
been essential for his rural reforms to be implemented. Third, the fiscal
resources available to the Uruguayan state from its burgeoning meat
and wool exports in the 1920s made the need for agrarian reform less
pressing or at least less apparent. Such an omission may be seen with
hindsight as a mistake or by neo-Marxist analysts as an inherent limitation
of Batlle's liberal vision. One can agree with Germán Rama that Batllismo
represented the rise of the middle class to political power in Uruguay
without condemning its ideology to the junk heap because of the possible
limitations of middle-class and reformist movements. The fact is that
the agrarian sector was not during Batlle's lifetime the bottleneck to
growth that it would be later on.

Batlle was, in spite of his rhetoric, no socialist. He sought to
mitigate the effects of Uruguay's dependence on foreign corporations at
the same time that he saw in a young and increasingly prosperous
Uruguay a real possibility of erecting a democratic polity firmly based
on social justice. It was a bold vision for a country of 1 million people
sandwiched between Argentina and Brazil. The problems of the 1960s
and beyond cast doubt on Batlle's legacy, and from a dependence theory
perspective Batllismo can be fairly criticized. As one critic has stated
the case,

> Basically, the Uruguay of 1911 had substantially the same problem as it
> has today. Its underdevelopment, although they did not use this word in
> that epoch, was determined by its structure and "English progress." It is
> known that a country can in no way progress beyond that which its least
> productive sector, be it agricultural or industrial, will permit. If the moment
> arrives in which agrarian production stagnates because it has reached the
> maximum development permitted by the latifundio, in the end, it produces
> stagnation throughout the service and industrial sectors. . . . Uruguay has
> been in this situation throughout this century, occasionally alleviated by
> the rise in prices produced by the world wars. In addition, between 1910

and 1915, immigration increased the population from one million to one and a quarter million in round numbers. How did Batlle handle these problems? He did not alter basic structures, but he did wind the national watch so that it could function rather well for some time. To achieve this, he took what we call a lateral road, for it passed alongside of structures without touching them. His policy consisted of creating a new investment sector, setting in motion the entrepreneurial state through interventionist politics. In this way, a series of state services were created and others nationalized, an impulse which will continue beyond his presidency and will be the soul of Batllista policy.[3]

CONSERVATIVE REACTION

Like all idea systems, Batllismo did not stand alone or unchallenged in Uruguay. It is not a surprise that the urban-oriented, prolabor welfare state liberalism of Batlle confronted a profoundly conservative counterideology that had its roots in the countryside.

Rural Uruguay always resented Montevideo, and that resentment turned to hatred under Batlle. Rural interests organized a new pressure group in the second decade of the twentieth century, partly as a response to the international economic climate and partly as a reaction to Batlle and his liberal, antireligious city. As Dr. José Irureta Goyena, a key leader of the Federación Rural, put it, "The idolatry of the factory does not permit the development of the religious life of the farm, as the fetishism of the city denies the noble cult of the countryside."[4]

With regard to religion, conservative Catholics certainly had good ground to oppose Batlle's atheism and his public policy of secularization of education, divorce, and holidays—all of which were part of what he called a program of *laicización*. These policies were never forgiven by the private Catholic school system. An indication of this is the fact that one of the most widely used secondary-school texts in that system called the socialism that Batlle "resolved to implement" in the country "irrealizable and disastrous."[5]

Conservative Catholics were not the only segment of society that felt Batllismo had moved the country too far to the left. Many attributed Batlle's defeat over the project to create a plural executive, the Colegiado, at the constitutional convention in 1916 to a rejection of more social and political engineering. Batlle managed to get a compromise over the Colegiado, but President Feliciano Rivera rallied the anti-Batllista Colorados with what is known in Uruguay as the *Alto de Rivera*, Rivera's halt:

The advanced economic and social laws sanctioned during the last legislative periods have alarmed many of our supporters, and it is they who have denied us their support in the elections of the thirtieth. Very well, gentlemen: we will not advance further in the area of social and economic legislation; we will reconcile capital and labor. We have moved too quickly; let us make a halt in the journey. We will not endorse new laws of this nature and we will shelve those that are being considered by the legislative body, or, at least, if they are sanctioned, it should be with the agreement of the parties directly involved.[6]

But Batlle's most powerful opponent was not from his own party. Luis Alberto de Herrera led the Blancos for much of the twentieth century and would outlive Batlle by thirty years, dying in 1959. A five-time candidate for president, he actually shared executive power first as a member of the National Council of Administration and then as the leader of the minority bloc in the purely collegial executive system by which the country was ruled under the 1952 constitution. Herrera had to live in a world of Batllista political and economic institutions, but he frequently maneuvered the system to his advantage, most notably during the 1933 coup, the new charters in 1934 and 1952, and the Blanco electoral victory in 1958.

Herrera was a patrician conservative, who supported the Axis during World War II, although his rationale was not so much a love of fascism as his fear of U.S. motives in South America. The bulk of his political energy was spent trying to dampen Colorado initiatives, as he himself offered no social programs during more than half a century of national political prominence. His conservatism on economic and social issues was compounded in later years by his growing anticommunism, which led in the 1950s to a successful political marriage with Benito Nardone and the Liga Federal de Acción Ruralista—the political movement known as Ruralismo.

Ruralismo was the brainchild of a conservative rancher, Juan Domingo R. Bordaberry, who started a newspaper called *Diario Rural* in 1940 and a successful radio station, Radio Rural, in 1951. Both media vehicles were run by Bordaberry's protégé, Benito Nardone, who quickly gained a large following of small ranchers and farmers. Nardone turned Ruralismo into the Uruguayan equivalent of the Poujadist movement in France on the basis of his strident anticommunism, attacks on urban liberalism, and his charismatic radio persona. He championed the *botudos*, the small farmers and ranchers, against the *galerudos*, the politicians and manufacturing interests of Montevideo. But his major rallying point was ideological—a religion-based anticommunism that took full advantage of the political climate of the 1950s. His newspaper essays and radio commentaries called for a vigilant struggle against the anti-Christian evils of Marxism. Batllismo was condemned for having brought the foreign ideas of socialism and anticlericalism into Uruguay. Batlle's legislation on the separation of church and state, civil divorce, and the secularization of religious holidays, as well as his exultation of the urban worker, was seen by Nardone as proof of his atheistic socialism.

Ruralismo's political adherents were not that large in number, but Nardone's alliance with the Blancos made the difference in their victory in the 1958 elections and helped the Partido Nacional hold on to its majority control of the Colegiado in 1962. The movement virtually disappeared as a mass organization after Nardone's death in 1964, although his widow and a powerful wool exporter, Juan José Gari, kept Radio Rural going. But this is not to say that the conservative, religious, anti-Communist and antistatist roots of the movement would not have an impact on future Uruguayan politics. In the 1971 elections, President Jorge Pacheco Areco personally chose as his successor the Colorado standard bearer and next president, Juan María Bordaberry. Bordaberry, son of Ruralismo founder Domingo Bordaberry, would turn out to be the military's willing partner in the *auto-golpe* that ended constitutional government in Uruguay in June 1973 and marked the beginning of a twelve-year dictatorship.

Some see the ultimate failure of Batllismo not in structural terms, but rather in the ease with which the movement succeeded—a deceptive ease that did not test or ripen a well-defined national character that would be conscious of the need for duty and sacrifice. This is how one of Uruguay's foremost historians, Carlos Real de Azúa, interprets it. For Azúa, Batlle inculcated economic nationalism into his program but failed to develop a sense of nationalism at the level of the individual. Following this analysis, Batllismo succeeded in vast areas of state-building and in some areas of constructing the social nation, including the creation of a commitment to democracy. But it did not succeed in inculcating a commitment to the nation that would make the state the "impersonal and ultimate arbiter in human affairs," as Kalman Silvert so aptly defined nationalism.[7] Lip service was paid after 1930 to Batlle's dream of a participant citizenry, and the weight of the institutions he created would continue to dominate political life, but the full bloom of the reciprocal loyalty between an impersonal state and an empathic citizenry would never emerge. One might blame this failure on the limits of liberalism or the power of dependence in a world economic system of international stratification. It may also be seen as the result of an underlying conflict between the values of the Batllista vision and a counterideology that finally had its opportunity to be implemented when economic crisis, social conflict, and political immobility ripped the constitutional fabric of the society.

THE ENDURING SYNTHESIS

Both parties were aware of the importance of public employment as the government made increasing use of the kinds of state enterprises favored by Batlle for two decades. The Colorados accepted these institutions as part of the Batllista vision. The Blancos accepted the creation of these *entes autónomos* with the hope they could be depoliticized, that is, removed from Colorado control. It was for these motivations that Article 100 of the constitution called for plural directorships of all state corporations, with directors chosen by the Consejo Nacional de Administración, thus ensuring minority representation by the Blancos in the directorship of the enterprises. Party, not nation, continued to be the vision that guided Uruguay's political class.

Public sector employment had doubled from 1900 to 1918 to an estimated 40,000 jobs. Control of the patronage inherent in this expanding public sector became the overriding consideration of both parties, especially as public employment increased by another 50 percent between 1920 and 1930 and a relative handful of votes—usually 5,000 to 10,000—separated the victorious Colorados from the always second-place Blancos. As one Colorado member of the Consejo described the work of the body:

> One will discuss whether, in accord with doctrine, the appointment of a janitor can be considered a party act, but as is public and notorious, that is exactly how it is considered. It is useless to pretend that the author of the declaration has wished to exclude from the so-called Colorado solutions precisely one which while not constituting the principal function of a government, is, definitively, the principal preoccupation of those that govern, to the point of making high administrative positions difficult and disagreeable.[8]

1929 was a bad year for the world and for Uruguay. October saw the crash of the stock market in New York and the death of José Batlle in Montevideo. The following year saw a precipitous decline in Uruguay's export earnings. In 1930 an anti-Batllista Colorado, Gabriel Terra, won the presidential election. Terra quickly used the economic crisis as a convenient excuse to attack much of the Batllista legacy including the collegial executive. He made an alliance with the Herrera wing of the Blanco party. Opposing factions (to Terra and Herrera) in both parties joined forces in a curious attempt to outmaneuver the president. The product of this dynamic was the creation of the largest state enterprise Uruguay has ever had and the most sectarian attempt to control the employment that would flow from its existence. The result would include the breakdown of constitutional rule.

At issue once again was the question of control of the state enterprises and their employment practices. Under a law passed in October 1931, all *entes autónomos* were to be controlled by a seven-member board of directors, and employment in each was to be based on party affiliation in a proportion determined by the relative showing of the two traditional parties in the previous election. The Blancos agreed to the creation of the enormous new state corporation ANCAP (Asociación Nacional de Combustibles, Alcohol y Portland), which would be responsible for the refining of all petroleum and for the production of alcohol and cement. In return, the Blancos were guaranteed control of part of the patronage that would flow from ANCAP. Thus, an institution that could be seen as a tribute to Batlle's vision of an economically autonomous and independent Uruguay became in reality something else. Jobs were being created and these jobs would be doled out not on the basis of merit or institutional need, and not even in fact by the two traditional parties as corporate entities, but by specific factions of each party. The agreement was quickly dubbed the Pacto de Chinchulín—the Pork Barrel Pact.

The agreement and the growing economic crisis brought on by the depression led to the first breakdown of constitutional rule since the 1903–1904 civil war. On March 31, 1933, Herrera supported President Terra's closing of parliament and declaration of emergency rule. Thus began what was to be known as the *dictablanda*, or soft dictatorship. The Terrista wing of the Colorados and the Herrerista Blancos then agreed to split public employment in the government bureaucracy and *entes autónomos* between their factions and put through a 1934 constitutional reform that returned the country to a presidential system and split the Senate fifty-fifty between the two groups. In essence the 1931 pact had been constitutionalized, but the victors of the spoils were now the factions that had been cut out in 1931.

As I observed in 1975, "One can argue that the real difference between the 1919 and 1934 constitutions was that in 1919 coparticipation was between the two traditional parties, but in the 1934 charter it was restricted to one faction from each of the parties. . . ."[9]

In return for supporting the coup, Herrera received further coparticipation in the new government by being guaranteed three of the nine ministerial portfolios. Similar mechanisms to ensure Herrerista input on the boards of state corporations were written into the 1934 charter. In essence, then, this document differed from the 1918 constitution, aside from the important return to presidential government, in the extent that the historic coparticipation of the two traditional parties was now limited to factions of each party. This restricted sharing of power was only possible under the mild dictatorship that characterized the regime. This peculiar governmental arrangement was made more palatable to the average Uruguayan by the economic emergency the country faced.

The election of 1938 brought Alfredo Baldomir and the Colorados a landslide victory, which made the new president less willing to accept the Herreristas as partners in government. The outbreak of World War II drove a further wedge into the 1924 alliance as Herrera was basically sympathetic to the Axis powers. Baldomir began to call for constitutional reform that would eliminate the special and exclusive coparticipation of the 1934 coup partners. When constitutional reform bogged down in delay and legal maneuvering, Baldomir engaged in a coup that had the support of all factions of the two traditional parties with the exception of the Herreristas. The coup resulted in the passage of the 1942 constitution, which codified the changes Baldomir wished to make. In essence, all political factions once again participated in political life and governmental patronage. With the export boom brought on by World War II and the industrialization it stimulated, Uruguay returned to the kind of economics and politics it had enjoyed in the 1920s. A not unexpected consequence of this process was the reinvigoration of the Batllista legacy. A principal benefactor of the rise of the new industrial bourgeoisie and burgeoning urban middle class, along with the vigorous growth of the urban working class, was Luis Batlle Berres, grandnephew of José Batlle.

Batlle Berres had succeeded to the presidency in 1947 upon the death of Tomás Barreta. In 1950 he led a clear-cut victory of his List 15 faction of the Colorado party over List 14, an increasingly conservative faction led by José Batlle's sons, Lorenzo and César, who were leading a passionate fight for the fulfillment of their father's dream of a completely collegial executive system (Colegiado Integral).[10]

Luis Batlle's election may not have sat well with the List 14 faction of the Colorados, but it was even more difficult for the old Blanco leader Luis Alberto de Herrera to accept. The 1950 election represented his sixth try for the presidency. He received 92,000 more votes than any other candidate, but with the electoral law known as the Ley de Lemas permitting the accumulation of votes by party factions (*sublemas*), the Colorados swamped the Blancos by 433,000 to 255,000. Herrera's only hope for a share of executive power now became the return to a collegial executive. He therefore did a complete about-face and supported Batlle's sons in their call for a constitutional convention to return the country to a collegial system of government. Lorenzo and César Batlle were more than happy to dilute Luis Batlle's power while fulfilling the historic goal of the Colegiado. The reform would not have passed without Herrera's support, as the proposal was defeated in Montevideo but was approved in the Blanco-dominated interior by a margin large enough to assure its passage.

The 1952 constitution created a nine-member executive with six seats going to the majority and three to the next most voted-for party—thus ensuring that either the Colorados or Blancos would get the minority seats on the Colegiado even if a third party should gain some public acceptance. The famous Pacto de Chinchulín, which had divided public employment among the traditional parties, was now written into the constitution; the five-member boards of all state enterprises were divided on a three-to-two basis between the two traditional parties.

Coparticipation had reached its fullest expression with the 1952 constitution. The two traditional parties were now dividing up a system that had grown fat during the boom years of World War II and the Korean War, which, fortunately for Uruguay (and unlike the Vietnam War), was fought in a cold climate necessitating wool uniforms. The country was prosperous, middle class, and its citizens enjoyed a high level of social services and welfare protection. This was Uruguay's golden era.

But the industrial populism practiced by Luis Batlle from 1948 on would now be tempered by shared executive authority and the onset of economic stagnation as import-substitution industrialization was quickly exhausted given Uruguay's small domestic market and low productivity. Uruguay's politicians would fiddle with their Colegiado and state corporations while Uruguay fell into economic stagnation, inflation, and a steadily devaluing currency.

The economic crisis was masked at first by dramatic political events. In 1958 the Blancos achieved their dream of controlling executive power in Uruguay, something they had not enjoyed for ninety-three years. With the aid of a weakening economy and the support of a neo-Fascist agrarian populist movement led by Benito Nardone, they swamped the Colorados in the elections. Everyone expected changes that would return the country to those economically bright days of the late 1940s and early 1950s, but this was not to be. Coparticipation meant that majority control of the executive could pass peacefully from Colorados to Blancos and that the Blancos would now control more patronage than the Colorados, but it did not mean that bold new economic or political initiatives would be forthcoming. It is unfortunate that the fact that the Blancos now had three seats on the directorship of state corporations instead of two was probably of more importance to citizens and politicians alike than the question of new policies to deal with the growing economic crisis. Coparticipation as an integrating mechanism was perverted by the sectarianism of party politics into jockeying for advantage by factions of the two traditional parties. What was left an orphan was the "national interest" and effective policies to promote it.

4

The Loss of Innocence: Crisis and Decline

A FLAWED POLITICAL ECONOMY

The stagnation that beset Uruguay from the mid-1950s on put an increasing burden on the public sector, both in terms of economic stimulation and employment. The state corporations encouraged by Batlle would be increasingly used by the political class to try to meet these needs. Some twenty-two *entes autónomos* generated some 30 percent of GDP (gross domestic product) and, by 1965, paid approximately 40 percent of all salaries. When the budgets of these corporations were added to the central government's expenditures, total government outlays represented 25 percent of GNP (gross national product). In addition to these burdens on the state was a retirement system that had to support over 270,000 pensioners in an economy that gainfully employed less than 1 million people.

The exhaustion of the import-substitution industrialization model had increased the insecurity of the middle class, thus placing a premium on the value given to being an *empleado público*. The traditional parties, through their control of the state bureaucracies, saw their future political well-being tied to the clamor for jobs and the supposed security that went with public employment. The political elite of both parties turned government into an employment office as they maneuvered for votes and legitimacy in an economy gone sour. The damage they did to the Uruguayan state in the process was aptly described by Aldo Solari, one of Uruguay's foremost sociologists: "Rather than as a secular artifact destined to resolve social conflicts at the highest level, the state is conceived in a paternalistic manner, as the one who must keep the vigil in order to, in the last analysis, sustain everyone. . . ."[1]

It is curious that the economic crisis in Uruguay had for several decades served to strengthen rather than diminish the power of the political elite. The stagnation of production that led to unemployment, inflation, and declining real income enhanced the role of the parties because they controlled the one expanding source of jobs—public employment.

The public sector absorbed some 40 percent of new jobs between 1955 and 1961 and 35 percent from 1961 to 1969. The GDP fell 5.4 percent in 1967 while inflation ran 89.3 percent. The following year GDP grew 1.1 percent and inflation hit a record high of 125.3 percent. From 1960 through 1965 only Malawi and the Dominican Republic had worse growth rates than Uruguay's, at .9 percent.

Mobility in Uruguay was a myth that died. Its demise would lead to increased social and political tensions that would put an end to Uruguay's exceptionalism in Latin America—the exceptionalism of a stable, middle-class democracy.

The 1960s had opened with gloom and sadness for Uruguay. The Blanco government that came to power in 1958 did not rekindle the economic flame and soon resorted to the same stopgap fiscal and monetary measures employed by the Colorados. At the time of the 1962 election, inflation was running at a historically high 35 percent. The Blancos managed to hold onto executive power, but their 120,000-vote margin in 1958 was reduced to only 24,000 in 1962.

As the economy continued to stagnate, so did political leadership. Several major political figures passed from the scene during this period. Luis Alberto de Herrera, the great Blanco caudillo, died in 1959 shortly after his party's electoral victory. Luis Batlle Berres, titular head of the liberal wing of the Colorado party, died in 1964, along with Benito Nardone, whose Ruralista movement had helped the Blancos to their breakthrough victory in 1958. Meanwhile, the cost of living, which had doubled between 1959 and 1962, doubled again in the following two years and went up another 100 percent in 1965 alone.

Professor Ronald H. McDonald summed up the deterioration of the Batllista legacy as follows:

> The old system is so sluggish and preoccupied with its traditional Montevideo electorate that creative leadership toward new development politics is precluded by short-run political sensitivities. These sensitivities have been bred by a half-century specialization on allocative rather than developmental public policy. The premise of Uruguayan political stability has been stable economic prosperity and irreversible growth. Developmental concerns effectively have been isolated from the political system, which works instead to redistribute and equalize income and affluence. The economically irrational effort at industrialization was but another subsidy to the welfare of the Montevideo voter, reallocating national wealth through

TABLE 4.1
Indicators of Internal Economic Activity, 1935-1967

Year	GDP	Consumer prices
1935-44	0.4	10.2
1945-54	3.8	6.8
1955-64	-1.4	22.3
1965	-0.1	56.5
1966	2.0	73.5
1967	-5.4	89.3

Source: Luis E. González and Jorge Notaro, "Alcances de una
Política Estabilizadora Heterodoxa: Uruguay 1974-1978," The
Wilson Center, Latin American Program, Working Papers, no. 45
(Washington, D.C., n.d.), p. 4.

inefficient, high cost industries producing consumer goods. As long as prosperity from exports continued, the system worked astonishingly well, producing one of Latin America's most stable and representative political systems.[2]

As usual, the reaction to the growing crisis was a call for constitutional reform. Now the politicians blamed the Colegiado for Uruguay's problems, arguing that a plural executive did not allow for the kind of quick and decisive decisionmaking called for by Uruguay's economic situation.

The populist Colorado leader, Luis Batlle Berres, warned his fellow citizens in 1962 that, "this country was the Switzerland of America, fundamentally because we worked, we produced and we sold. We could stop being the Switzerland of America in the political and social realms if we continue feeling this ever deepening wound to our economy."[3] Indeed the economic record of these years was less than enviable, as indicated by the data in Table 4.1. Opinion polls show that the public understood the arguments in favor of what was to be the 1966 constitutional reform, but that support for a return to a presidential system depended on the respondents' economic circumstances and eroded as one descended the socioeconomic ladder.

The 1966 constitutional reform was a nuts-and-bolts political affair devoid of the kind of philosophical debate that accompanied the previous changes in the governing charter of Uruguay. It is clear that there was an effort at reform in the return to a presidential system and the adoption of certain administrative changes in the retirement and social security systems, as well as in the creation of a central bank. In addition, an attempt was made to improve the technical capacity of the executive branch through the establishment of an Office of Planning and Budget.

As we shall see, however, even these positive steps would prove inadequate in the face of a governing class unable or unwilling to take the necessary steps to confront the growing crisis.

The constitution was easily passed in a plebiscite held concurrently with the 1966 elections. The Colorado party won easily and President Oscar Gestido, a retired general known for his administrative capability and honesty, was inaugurated. But it would be his vice president, Jorge Pacheco Areco, a little-known newspaper editor and minor party activist, who would leave an indelible mark upon Uruguay. Pacheco succeeded to the presidency in 1968 upon the death of Gestido, who had been in office less than a year. Within a week after taking office, Pacheco issued a decree outlawing the Socialist party and several small anarchist and leftist groups. The Socialist party's newspaper, *El Sol*, and the independent leftist newspaper, *Epoca*, were permanently closed.

To implement the new monetarist policy adopted in 1968, Alejandro Végh Villegas was installed as director of the recently created Office of Planning and Budget. (Végh would go on to play a crucial role during the dictatorship, as minister of economy from 1974 to 1976 and again from late 1983 to February of 1985.) The June 1968 economic decree freezing wages and prices was a concession to the IMF's (International Monetary Fund) interpretation of inflation as the product of excess demand provoked by credit expansion, fiscal deficits, and salary increases. To administer the program, a new body was established—COPRIN, the Comisión de Productividad, Precios y Ingresos (Commission for Productivity, Prices, and Wages). Initially the program had some success, especially in dealing with inflation. Consumer prices rose by an average of 25 percent annually between 1969 and 1971. However, as the November 1971 elections approached, the government increased spending. This resulted in a fiscal deficit of 30 percent, which was compounded by a negative trade balance.

Pacheco justified his actions as president, which included the drafting of striking bank workers in 1968, on the basis of the growing threat from the guerrilla movement. The dialectic of increased repression and increased guerrilla activity would lead Uruguay on a path that would continually weaken the constitutional norms and safeguards for which the country had been justly praised.

THE BREAKDOWN OF DEMOCRACY

On June 13, 1968, the government instituted a limited state of siege by invoking emergency powers granted by the constitution under the so-called Medidas Prontas de Seguridad (Prompt Security Measures). With the exception of a brief period during 1969, Pacheco governed under these measures for his remaining four years in office. Furthermore, parliament would twice acquiesce in the suspension of all civil liberties, once for twenty days following the assassination in August 1970 of U.S. police agent Daniel Mitrione and then for forty days following the January 1971 kidnapping of British ambassador Jeoffrey Jackson—both by the MLN-Tupamaros (Movimiento de Liberación Nacional; National Liberation Movement). All of the above measures were justified in terms of the government's struggle against this guerrilla organization.

The Tupamaros were organized in 1963 around a nucleus of disenchanted members of the Socialist party. The movement's leader, Raúl Sendic, was a thirty-six-year-old law student and party activist who had organized sugar workers in Uruguay's Northeast. He and his followers had grown increasingly disillusioned with a peaceful path to change in Uruguay and decided to organize and train clandestinely with the aim of eventually challenging the political and governmental institutions of the society. The National Liberation Movement took on the additional name "Tupamaros," adopting the term from the Inca chieftain Tupac Amaru who fought the Spanish conquistadores in Peru at the end of the eighteenth century.

The guerrillas took several years to organize and arm themselves, finally declaring their existence to their fellow citizens in a 1967 statement, which made their position and motives clear:

> For these reasons, we have placed ourselves outside the law. This is the only honest action when the law is not equal for all; when the law exists to defend the spurious interests of a minority in detriment to the majority; when the law works against the country's progress; when even those who have created it place themselves outside it, with impunity, whenever it is convenient for them.
>
> The hour of rebellion has definitively sounded for us. The hour of patience has ended. The hour of action and commitment has commenced here and now. The hour of conversation and enunciation of theory, propositions and unfulfilled promises is finished.
>
> We should not be worthy Uruguayans, nor worthy Americans, nor worthy of ourselves if we do not listen to the dictates of conscience that day after day calls us to the fight. Today no one can take the sacred right of rebellion away from us, and no one is going to stop us from dying, if necessary, in order to be of consequence.[4]

The Tupamaro slogan during its successful and most active period from 1969 to 1972 was *"Habrá patria para todos o patria para nadie"* (There will be a fatherland for all or a fatherland for none). Unfortunately, the Tupamaros would help create the latter.

The Tupamaros first benefited from and then were victimized by the Uruguayan penchant for myth making. Extolling them for their efficiency, wit, and Robin Hood image, Uruguayans seemed proud of the fact that their guerrillas were the best in Latin America. After the Mitrione assassination, this image faded badly. Daniel Mitrione was a retired police chief from Muncie, Indiana, who was employed by the Office of Public Safety of the U.S. Agency for International Development (USAID). He worked out of police headquarters in Montevideo. The Tupamaros, as well as others, regarded Mitrione as a CIA agent who was involved in, or supported the use of, torture in order to obtain countersubversive information. He was kidnapped on July 31, 1970. The Tupamaros demanded the release of all guerrilla prisoners as a condition for his ransom. Apparently a deal was about to be made when Uruguayan police intelligence units captured the leadership of the Tupamaros as they met to discuss their next step in the ransom talks. The Pacheco government now stiffened its position, and talks broke off. On August 8, Mitrione's body was discovered in an abandoned automobile. The struggle between the Tupamaros and the government had now escalated dangerously.

With the onset of the military dictatorship, Uruguayan public opinion began to blame the Tupamaros for the loss of democracy, a position still held by many. In fact, the Tupamaros were never as adept (politically, ideologically, or tactically) as the public believed and cannot be "blamed" for the dictatorship. The record shows that civil liberties had been seriously eroded under Pacheco Areco. In addition, torture had become an accepted police practice. As one parliamentary investigation concluded,

> The application of tortures in different forms is a normal, frequent, and habitual occurrence and that, among officials of recognized abilities, individuals have infiltrated who use their public positions to give free rein to their perverse instincts. It is also clear that the High Command lacks energy and courage, if it is not at times an accomplice, in transforming the prisons into places where the human being undergoes tortures incompatible with our democracy, our style of life and degree of civilization.[5]

Alejandro Otero, head of the police intelligence unit—the Information and Intelligence Directorate—in charge of the struggle against the Tupamaros, was considered too liberal when he went on record as opposed to torture and brutal treatment of suspects and prisoners. He was fired in January of 1970.

The guerrillas must share responsibility for the escalating violence that increased the role and hence the political influence of the armed forces in Uruguay, but they cannot be saddled with the blame for the theories and practices that were employed by Uruguay's rulers from 1973 until 1984.

On September 9, 1971, after the spectacular escape of over 100 Tupamaros from Punta Carretas Penitentiary, President Pacheco put the armed forces in charge of all antiguerrilla activity. The effect of this move was not immediate because the guerrillas soon called a truce in the months surrounding the November 1971 elections. This informal truce ended violently on April 14, 1972, when the Tupamaros assassinated several officials in various sectors of Montevideo and lost several of their own members in the ensuing skirmishes with police and army personnel. President Bordaberry immediately asked for, and received, a declaration of "internal war." In reality Uruguay was under martial law, with the suspension of all constitutionally guaranteed individual liberties.

In hindsight, the decision to refrain from their usual activities from October 1971 until April 1972 was a fatal mistake for the Tupamaros. Apparently wanting to broaden their base, the movement took a calculated risk and supported the Frente Amplio (Broad Front), the leftist electoral coalition, in the elections. But the Tupamaros never believed that fundamental change was going to be made in Uruguay through the ballot box. Their own existence may be explained, in part, by the frustration this generation felt about electoral politics, the conservative nature of Uruguayan society, and the bleak future they faced economically. When the Tupamaros finally reescalated in April, they faced a firmly entrenched administration backed by an increasingly well equipped and adequately prepared military that had finally been given a blank check to get rid of the problem. The armed forces needed only three months to crush the guerrilla movement—a movement that had by now totally estranged itself from public opinion and was isolated from the liberal and leftist groups it had surfaced to support during the election.

Luis Costa Bonino saw the ideological and military disintegration of the Tupamaros as stemming from the loss (albeit temporary) of the first generation of leadership in the arrests that took place during the Mitrione kidnapping in August 1970.[6] He persuasively argued that the older generation of Tupamaros were the "politicians" of the movement, who had a vision of a national identity reinvigorated by socialism. The generation that took over when these individuals were captured were the "soldiers" of the movement. They were more dogmatic, rigid, and myopic and would guide the organization into the tactical and public relations errors that would lead to the strategic disaster they encountered in mid-1972. It is true that the old leaders did escape from prison in September 1972, but by then, according to Costa Bonino, the organization was committed to an escalation that would lead to direct confrontation with the armed forces.

The first generation created the MLN-Tupamaros, whereas the new leadership had been nurtured and socialized by the group in an atmosphere of clandestine and escalating guerrilla activity. Only the original leadership had a political role in the movement; the new recruits were foot soldiers, who, in an increasingly ugly confrontation suddenly found themselves in a position of authority.

For Luis Costa Bonino, the Tupamaros were doomed from the start. Their project may have stemmed from a nationalist vision, but their demand for fundamental change and the "heroic" attitude they adopted to accomplish it was ultimately rejected by an Uruguayan society dominated by the middle-class love affair with security. Threatened at first by economic insecurity and later by the political struggle between the Tupamaros and the security forces, the average Uruguayan retreated into an acquiescence in the destruction of the Tupamaros and a similar inaction in the face of the erosion and final destruction of constitutional government.

The 1971 election was a watershed in Uruguayan politics. The incumbent president, Jorge Pacheco Areco, sought reelection via a constitutional amendment to be plebiscited concurrently with the election. At the same time, he handpicked the Colorado party's regular candidate, Juan María Bordaberry, from a conservative ranching family. Among the Blancos, Senator Wilson Ferreira Aldunate, emerged as a major figure, but his liberal position on many issues did not sit well with the traditionally conservative factions of his party.

The Frente Amplio was born of an amalgam of Uruguay's traditional leftist parties—Communist and Socialist—and the addition of a few leftist factions of the Blanco and Colorado parties, most notably Colorados Zelmar Michelini (List 99) and Alba Roballo. Blanco Senator Francisco Rodríguez Camusso (List 1051) was the principal defection from the Partido Nacional. The Frente was organized in 1970, taking its inspiration from the success of Salvador Allende's Unidad Popular in Chile. In order to accumulate votes under the Ley de Lemas and the 1966 constitution, the various factions needed to run under the aegis of a "permanent" party. The Christian Democratic party, headed by Juan Pablo Terra, lent its party title (lema) to the coalition, thus enabling it to contest the election; the votes of its various constituents were accumulated under the legal designation of the Christian Democratic party, but with the popular identification as the Frente Amplio.

The Frente captured a disappointing 18 percent of the national vote. But in Montevideo it confirmed what most observers thought was true of the Left—that it was a viable third party in the capital, capturing

30 percent of the vote there. The Frente could aspire to winning the *Intendencia* of the Department of Montevideo, which is one of the most powerful elected positions in the country. It is worth noting that the same electoral laws that were created and used by the Blancos and Colorados to keep their electoral strength intact, by allowing accumulation of votes by the various intraparty factions, were eventually used to make a leftist coalition possible.

The campaign took place amidst increasing violence and polarization, but not from the Tupamaros, who had called a truce for the election. Physical attacks were made on General Liber Seregni, the nonaligned retired general who was the sole presidential candidate for the Frente Amplio. Newspapers warned that a vote for the Frente was a vote for the Russian bear. Two days prior to the election, conservative Blancos and Colorados participated in a large demonstration in "defense of democracy." To his credit, Senator Ferreira, who had emerged as the most liberal among the eight presidential candidates of the two traditional parties, asked his supporters to remain home and not participate in the demonstration.

The election itself turned out to be one of the most controversial in Uruguay's history. A large turnout was assured by the government's decision to enforce the obligatory voting clause in the constitution. A late spring heat wave did not help the long lines of voters already inconvenienced by procedural delays that required the government to obtain a four-hour extension in voting hours. But the vote count itself quickly overshadowed the difficulties during the campaign.

Early returns revealed the expected pattern: a heavy Colorado plurality in Montevideo with the customary Blanco advantage in the interior. But attention quickly turned to the narrowing Colorado lead when, with half the votes counted, the Colorado plurality fell below 11,000. Because the late returns from the traditionally Blanco dominated interior were still to be counted, a Wilson (as Senator Wilson Ferreira Aldunate is commonly known in Uruguay) victory looked more and more probable. But after a mysterious halt in the vote count, the Colorado lead held and Juan María Bordaberry was declared the unofficial winner. Wilson turned out to have the most votes—26 percent of the total to Bordaberry's 24 percent—but the Colorados outpolled the Blancos by some 13,000 votes, thus assuring a Bordaberry presidency under Uruguay's electoral laws.

As I wrote about this election in a previous work,

> Wilson Ferreira Aldunate was prevented from winning the election by a determined Colorado president and the acquiescence of conservative Blancos who did not wish to see their own party's liberal presidential

candidates elected, even if it meant that their party was defeated. There is strong evidence to support this view beyond the irregularities mentioned above. The amending ballot supporting Pacheco's reelection was deliberately almost identical to the regular Bordaberry ballot. Voting procedures enabled the citizens to put both the ballot for amendment and his regular election ballot in the same envelope. Given the large number of reform ballots cast (several hundred thousand), it is not difficult to believe that several thousand Pacheco ballots found their way into the regular Colorado tally. (One observer estimated that some 35,000 extra ballots could have been credited to Bordaberry in this manner, over two and one-half times more than the winning margin.)[7]

It should also be noted that Pacheco's unsuccessful attempt at reelection got him more votes than any candidate in the history of Uruguay. This was a strong indication of the popularity of his tough law-and-order stance.

THE END OF DEMOCRACY

The Bordaberry administration continued the policies of its predecessor. The Uruguayan government's priorities were reflected in its budget. Between 1968 and 1973 the education component of the budget fell from 24.3 to 16.6 percent, while the military component increased from 13.9 to 26.2 percent. (The dictatorship's preoccupation with security would subsequently push army and police expenditures to over 40 percent of the central government budget.) In addition, Bordaberry proposed legislation to eliminate university autonomy and enhance the powers of the army and police. Nevertheless, the military grew impatient with civilian rule. It was now time for the armed forces' final assault on the Uruguayan polity.

The military's most significant challenge to presidential authority occurred during the second week in February 1973, when the army and air force rebelled against President Bordaberry's selection of Antonio Francese as minister of defense. This skirmish quickly turned into a quasi-coup. The military was demonstrating its intention to oversee national policy. Bordaberry managed to stay in office, but policy was now to be supervised by a newly created National Security Council (COSENA; Consejo de Seguridad Nacional) dominated by the military. This period, known as "Bitter February," is considered by most observers to be the beginning of a drawn-out coup that culminated at the end of June.

The military now pushed for the final approval and implementation of draconian national security regulations. Parliamentary reluctance to go along with such measures, as well as President Bordaberry's loss of a legislative majority because of the defection of several legislators, caused the military to issue several communiqués denouncing the nation's politicians for being soft on the war against subversion. When parliament refused to lift the immunity of Senator Enrique Erro, whom the military charged with complicity with the Tupamaros, and voted to investigate charges of torture leveled against the armed forces, the generals decided that they had had enough. On June 27, 1973, President Bordaberry, backed by the military, closed Parliament, prohibited the dissemination of any information implying dictatorial motives to the government, and empowered the police and armed forces to take whatever measures were necessary to ensure normal public services.

The dictatorship was launched. Its record of arrests, torture, and murder, combined with its actions against unions, the university, the press, and all forms of culture undertaken in the concentrated and intimate world that is Montevideo, established a regime that was to be the most totalitarian on the continent.

The coup in Uruguay was a drawn-out affair. It was thus far less dramatic than its counterpart in Chile. Perhaps the actions taken by Bordaberry and the military would have received more attention if Allende had not been overthrown on September 11 of the same year. The international preoccupation with events in Chile afforded the Uruguayan dictatorship the luxury of silence and anonymity, which allowed it to act with impunity while creating a totalitarian regime in a nation that had traditionally been even more democratic and civil than Chile.

As we shall see in Chapter 5, the systematic but "constitutional" attack conducted by Pacheco and Bordaberry on the guerrillas, the press, the unions, and the university would be extended and refined by the military. With no constitutional safeguards or anything remotely resembling the rule of law, there was only one rule—force—and it was carried out by the military in its paranoid quest for national security. As Rear Admiral Francisco Sangurgo succinctly put it while defending the dictatorship's human rights record, "Before they criticize our Armed Forces so harshly, they ought to take a look at what happens to those plutocratic democracies that wave the flag of ideological pluralism and peaceful co-existence . . . [for] in spite of itself liberal democracy leads to communism."

To understand the final breakdown of constitutional rule, we must examine one more factor—labor. Labor was basically moderate in Uruguay for the first five decades of the century. There were several reasons for this stance. In the first place, unionized workers were only a small percentage of the urban population and most factories were small, employing fewer than fifty people. Equally as important, the Batllista welfare state had systematically ameliorated worker demands. But from 1956 to 1972 the GNP fell 12 percent, and in the decade from 1957 to

1967 real wages for public employees fell 40 percent. The result was increased labor unrest. Man-days lost to strikes increased from an average of 1.2 million annually in the 1950s to 2.5 million in 1963.[8] In 1966 a national labor organization dominated by the Communist party and known as the National Federation of Workers (CNT; Convención Nacional de Trabajadores) was established.

The first "state of siege" was imposed during growing labor unrest in 1965. As the conflict between labor and government intensified, the government response escalated. During 1969 hundreds of labor union leaders and activists were arrested and reports of beatings and torture began to surface. In the midst of the debate on the government plan to draft striking bank workers, Defense Minister Antonio Francese appeared before a legislative committee and declared, "I am not here as a minister, but as a General; the armed forces are the guardians of the nation's institutions."[9] By July 1969 the CNT leadership was operating out of a clandestine headquarters. When in August of that year the parliament rescinded the military draft of striking bank employees, President Pacheco simply reissued it and parliament reluctantly acquiesced. There would be further acquiescence by parliament that would erode constitutional safeguards. Pacheco was allowed to reimpose a state of siege almost at will throughout his presidency; when he declared a state of "internal war" in April of 1972, which was supposed to last for thirty days, the legislature permitted it to continue into 1973.

In Howard Handelman's survey of Uruguayan industrialists conducted in 1976, some 52 percent indicated that "control of labor unrest" was the major accomplishment of Uruguay's military government, and many who saw the guerrillas as the major problem felt the country had been engulfed in a leftist conspiracy framed by the Tupamaros and labor strife.[10] The Ley de Seguridad del Estado (State Security Law) (Ley de Orden Público No. 14,068) was approved by parliament, with the support of the two traditional parties, on July 10, 1972. This legislation in effect gave juridical recognition to the suspension of individual liberties and the violent repression that had been conducted by the military under the declaration of a state of internal war. This legislation would also become the juridical rationale for the dictatorship's actions and is constantly alluded to by the military when the human rights theme is discussed. Again, in February 1973, except for a few lonely voices, parliament did nothing to oppose the military's imposition of a National Security Council (COSENA) on the executive branch, even though this action marked the direct entry of the armed forces into the institutional political structure of the country.

Professor Ronald H. McDonald has conceptualized the military's growing political role in the following scheme:

As the traumatic decade from 1964 to 1974 is reconstructed, there appear to have been several distinct stages of military involvement, moving in the single direction toward greater participation in government decision-making and administration. As the sequence progressed, each stage ended with a crisis, either prompting the military toward greater involvement, or in turn prompted by internal divisions within the military over the issue of escalating involvement. The sequence might be conceptualized as follows: a period of growing concern about civil disobedience, but publicly a low profile (1964–1966); publicly expressed concern about the Tupamaro threat, the national institutions' and leaders' capacity and determination to respond, and increasing pressure on government leaders (1967–1971); assumption of direct responsibility for internal security; substitution of military for civil procedures and protections, and direct attacks on public and government leaders and institutions (1971–1972); indirect control over the government through the President (1972–1973); and finally, in February with the attempted coup, and later in June, 1973, imposition of direct, formal control over the highest decision-making institution, the presidency, and dissolution of its principal check, the legislature. Unlike Chile, where the military came to power in a few short hours, the process of dismantling the Uruguayan political system extended for almost a decade, but with the same result.[11]

As has been argued in this chapter, there were several reasons for this spiral into dictatorship. Economic decline, social unrest, and terrorism played their parts. But one of the great dilemmas of Uruguay in the 1950s and 1960s was the fact that, for the most part, there were parties without intellectuals and intellectuals without parties. This state of affairs contributed to "the transformation of the politician into a superintendent, the division of the parties into a multitude of small groups, the loss of internal democracy and the predominance of personalism, [which] resulted in the inability of political parties to elaborate programs and the loss of the capacity to articulate any kind of alternative political response."[12]

Uruguay lost its democracy and no group could escape without some blame for the ensuing decade of terror, despair, and opportunity lost.

5
The Military Dictatorship

Uruguay's armed forces were always separated from civilian society. This marginalization extended to recruitment patterns. The officer corps was recruited from the lower middle class residing in the small towns and cities of the interior, whereas the troops came from the lowest strata of the rural sector, usually former peons from the ranches or unemployed workers from the slums surrounding urban areas.

The military was considered marginal to political life in Uruguay, ignored by politicians and academics alike. In 1965, Uruguay ranked 91st of 121 countries in terms of the percentage of GNP devoted to the military. During the 1960s there were 21,500 individuals in the military: 17,000 in the army, 2,000 in the air force, and 2,500 in the navy. In addition, 17,000 were in the country's police forces. The number of personnel in military uniform grew precipitously during the 1970s, from slightly over 21,000 in 1970, to 38,500 in 1978. When the forces, mostly police, under the Ministry of Interior are added, the total for all security forces was over 64,000 in 1978 and was still close to 59,000 in 1984. From 1946 to 1982, 920 Uruguayan officers attended courses at Fort Gulick in the Panama Canal Zone. Their training and ideological indoctrination evolved from an external defense mission to one of internal security and counterterrorism, although they were not asked to directly assume this role in Uruguay until September 1971, when they were put in direct charge of the struggle against the Tupamaros. After having destroyed the guerrillas in a relatively few months, the military turned its attention to the question of the future of the Uruguayan state—its cleansing and reordering.

POLITICAL ORIENTATION

The armed forces were first seen as a possible source of progressive change—à la Peru—because of Communiqués 4 and 7 that were issued in February of 1973 to justify the military's assertion of veto power over the Bordaberry government.

Some sectors on the Left, most conspicuously the Communist party, saw a potentially nationalist and reformist military, that is, one which takes power in a spirit of reform, not repression. Consequently, they did not oppose the armed forces' challenge to civilian authority in February and abandoned the general strike that took place at the beginning of the dictatorship in late June and early July 1973 in the hope they could negotiate with the military. This proved to be an error.

The author of Communiqués 4 and 7 was Colonel Ramón Trabal, who was mysteriously assassinated in Paris in December 1974. These communiqués proved in retrospect to be either the clever public relations of a politically activated military or merely the wishful thinking of part of the Uruguayan Left, most especially the Communist party. In fact, the military was not falling under the sway of progressive-minded officers, as in the Peru of 1968, but rather under the control of those most intimately involved in the struggle against the Tupamaros and those most infatuated by the idea of a *partido militar*. These men sought to save the country not so much from the guerrillas, who were never that significant a military threat and in any event had been destroyed by late 1972, but from the liberal Batllista legacy that had nurtured the Left, grown corrupt, and had ultimately proven itself incapable of overcoming Uruguay's economic crisis. As Juan Rial summarized this period,

> Given the fact that the country found itself in a high degree of inertia, with a stalemate between the various social and political forces that were incapable of proposing a new style in order to adapt to change and a new international environment, it quickly became evident that perhaps the only place where these blockages could be reflected upon and perhaps resolved was the armed forces. Their strong autonomy from civil society, their statist character, their dependence on the survival of the state, and the fact that Uruguayan civil society was weak and subordinated to a paternalistic State, made the task easier.[1]

In January of 1985 a former high-ranking officer, Brigadier Jorge Borad, indicated that the communiqués were hurriedly drafted as a public relations ploy and that was the reason they included a discussion of the need for land reform and other progressive changes. The real mission of the military quickly became apparent. The aim was to destroy all forms of subversion in order to preserve the Uruguayan state. This required actions that went far beyond the mere destruction of the Tupamaro guerrillas, but the destruction of the guerrillas was seen as fundamental to the preservation of the state.

Bastaron no más de siete meses para que el aparato sedicioso, brazo armado de la subversión, fuera destrozado por una acción militar lo necesariamente energica y coherente como para reestablecer la confianza que el Estado, durante años de desidia y politiqueria, habia venido perdiendo progresivamente como instrumento de orden, de paz y de progreso.

[No more than seven months were needed both for the seditionary apparatus, an armed extension of subversion, to be destroyed by a necessarily energetic and coherent military action and to reestablish the credibility that the state had been progressively losing as an instrument of order, peace, and progress during years of indolence and petty politicking.][2]

Uruguay under military rule was not a history of a *líder máximo*. The armed forces, perhaps out of mutual distrust, chose to rule through a series of bureaucratic institutions. If there was a pyramid of power, it certainly did not culminate in one man. The military never developed a charismatic "first among equals" in their ranks at any time during the dictatorship. Mandatory retirement was strictly followed as was the transfer of various military commands. General Gregorio Alvarez did try to turn himself into Uruguay's Pinochet after he assumed the presidency in 1978 but did not succeed.

The bureaucratic nature of military rule began with the creation of the COSENA, which was established to oversee presidential decisions in February 1973. The council consisted of the heads of the three branches of the armed forces and the ministers of defense, interior, foreign affairs, and the economy, along with the president. After the coup in June of 1973, several new bodies were created by the armed forces. In 1976, a Council of the Nation was established that consisted of the twenty-five civilians who made up the Council of State (originally set up to replace the closed parliament) and twenty-one generals of the armed forces—the Junta of Generals. The armed forces also set up a Commission on Political Affairs (Comisión de Asuntos Políticos; COMASPO) and a military publicity service known as DINARP (Dirección Nacional de Relaciones Públicas). Real power, however, was held by the military and especially the commanders of the three armed services who formed an informal body known as the Junta de Comandantes en Jefe (Junta of Commanders in Chief). In the waning years of the dictatorship, the COMASPO would take on increased importance as it presented projects and negotiated with the civilian opposition.

NATIONAL SECURITY DOCTRINE AND THE DICTATORSHIP

Under the doctrine of national security, the twin requirements of security and development are imposed from outside the social system.

They are garbed in a pseudoscientific analysis of society grounded in geopolitics. Sovereignty no longer resides in the people, but derives from the requirements of state survival. National security doctrine thus becomes an updated version of the theological justification for rule.

Uruguay's military shares the ideology of national security made famous by the Brazilian generals after their takeover in 1964. The core of the doctrine is exemplified by Brazilian General Golbery do Couto e Silva in his book *Geopolítica do Brasil.* Essentially the book describes a world divided into two opposing blocs, the capitalist Christian West and the Communist atheistic East, each with its own values that are considered irreconcilable. The Latin generals see themselves as part of the Western bloc and are therefore engaged in an unrelenting global struggle with the opposition. This struggle calls for a war in which there is no room for hesitation or uncertainty against a cunning and ruthless enemy. Thus, it is necessary to sacrifice some secular freedoms in order to protect and preserve the state.

According to this doctrine, the military plays an active role in the economic and political affairs of the country and seeks to permanently ensure its intervention through law and the institutions of the state. The doctrine of national security has both secular and religious components. The sacred takes the form of an almost religious or holy war against "Communist subversion," whereas the secular involves a reordering of economic policies and priorities so as to ensure development, without which the instability that originally provoked the military's intervention would presumably return.

The struggle against subversion had its most dramatic moment in Uruguay during the height of the guerrilla movement, which achieved its most spectacular successes between 1968 and 1971. But the declaration of internal war in April 1972 led to the destruction of the Tupamaros within a few months. However, the almost religious struggle against the subversive menace had only just begun. The outlawing of the Communist-led National Federation of Workers on June 30, 1973, was, from the military's point of view, a second great blow against subversion. With armed insurrection destroyed and the union organizations outlawed, the military turned its attention to what it saw as subversion by intellectuals in the schools and the university. In September 1975, when a student was killed in an explosion at the University of the Republic, the military occupied various university buildings and arrested the rector and all the deans of the various facilities, with the exception of Alberto Pérez Pérez, dean of the Law School, who was in Buenos Aires at the time and would spend the next eleven years in exile. In December, the Communist and Socialist parties and the student federation (FEUU) were banned and members of these organizations arrested. The moves against parties and educational institutions led to the mass arrest of political and intellectual activists.

In a remarkable book that is a justification to the Uruguayan people for their assumption of power, the commanders in chief of the armed forces made the following comment on world history: "The renewed communism of the Bolshevik Revolution of October 1917 constitutes, in the events of this century, the direct or indirect, visible or obscured, source of the subversion in the world today."[3] In this volume, "national security" is defined as "the means whereby the national heritage in any form and the development process, bearing national objectives in view, are protected from internal or external interference." Following in this vein, the national heritage is deemed to include the political and social structure, traditions, history, and culture. The logic is inescapable: The military has to supervise all aspects of political, economic, and social life in the country.

The struggle against subversion required a particular military action that was within the competence of the armed forces. That accomplished, the military concluded that subversion had its roots in the social, economic, educational, and moral structures of society and sought to extirpate these roots as a legitimate part of their mission. The national security state was the apparatus through which this task was to be accomplished.

The managers of this system do not guide policy by balancing a democratic game of give-and-take but rather operate according to a management scheme in which the data are derived from an analysis of Communist ideology and geopolitical "reality." Under such a system, human rights quickly became superfluous. When this concept is married to an organic concept of the state, an indefinite prolongation of emergency rule is justified because communism is a form of permanent aggression. Liberalism is viewed as leading to communism because it creates a skeptical secular person incapable of standing up to the holy war on communism. The liberal framework of law simply cannot cope with subversion. The fight against subversion can only be won by marrying the concepts of security and development, and this can only be done through the erection of the national security state.[4]

Creating a totalitarian state requires people and resources. As indicated, the total number of military and police personnel (the police were under military control during the dictatorship) grew from some 42,000 in 1970 to over 64,000 in 1978. In 1983, 49 percent of the central government budget went to the Ministries of Defense and Interior. This sum was 7.7 percent of GDP and represented 30 percent of all public sector expenditures.

THE MILITARY AND HUMAN RIGHTS

In comparison to the Argentine or Chilean experience, the number of deaths related to the military dictatorship is low. Best estimates are that approximately ninety persons died during torture, 44 disappeared in Uruguay, and 123 disappeared in Argentina, apparently as the result of joint actions of Argentine and Uruguayan security personnel. The military did not rule by killing. As Reverend Luis Pérez Aguirre, head of Servicio Paz y Justicia (SERPAJ; Peace and Justice Service), the most important human rights group in Uruguay, aptly summarized the dictatorship, "Uruguay did not have the most blood-thirsty regime, but it was the most totalitarian through its use of fear and terror to demobilize the population."[5]

The methods of torture were not new. They included electric shock, beatings, sensory deprivation, simulated executions and drownings, and the gang raping of a woman in front of her husband and/or children. In one case a man had rubber ropes gradually tightened across his thighs. The torturers felt they would thus leave no trace of their activities, but the process killed all the hair follicles, a condition that has no known medical cause and thus enabled the physicians to verify the individual's testimony.[6]

Children disappeared in Uruguay during the dictatorship, just as they did in Argentina. The numbers were much smaller than in Argentina, but in several instances children who happened to be present at the time their parents were arrested were taken away by security forces and were never returned to their families. Usually they were placed for adoption outside of Uruguay. Some of these children have subsequently turned up in Brazil and in Chile. In one case, a mother was told she could have her child back and her sentence reduced if she would name names. She refused and never saw her child again.

The military instituted an infamous "ABC" system whereby every adult was investigated and then given a letter designation of his or her "democratic faith" based on the record. Those who fell into the "C" category were denied public employment and would not be issued passports. Having been a member of a banned political or student group, even if this had occurred twenty years earlier and the group had then been legal and law-abiding, was sufficient cause for placement in the "C" category. Being designated a "B" meant you were of questionable loyalty and therefore would be watched carefully. Only those in the "A" category were considered safe and "good" citizens.

On December 29, 1975, the government, using the 1972 State Security Law as its basis, declared that all persons charged with crimes under that law, regardless of the date of such crimes, would be subject to military courts and military justice. In May of 1975, the director of secondary education ordered school authorities to eliminate from school libraries all books, magazines, newspapers, brochures, and records whose content "did not conform to the fundamental principles of the nation, particularly when they followed a Marxist line." Uruguay's security forces would arrest and detain over 60,000 citizens. In 1979 Amnesty International estimated that one in fifty Uruguayans had been through some period of imprisonment.

The military's *modus operandi* has been eloquently captured by Juan Corradi in a superb essay on Argentina that is also relevant to the situation in Uruguay.

> The public arena, the previous mechanisms of representation, all free discursive exchanges have disappeared. Subjects are no longer interpellated by and recognize themselves in a familiar central Subject (Class, Government, Party). The state withdraws from the public sphere to ensconce itself in the old *arcana dominationis* from whence it arbitrarily strikes in inappellable ways. To the underlying population, punishment arrives like the unfathomable act of a *deus absconditus*. They have to work out for themselves, like latter-day political Calvinists—the rules, the signs, that distinguish a "good" from a "bad" citizen. All they know is that their safety, their goods, their lives, are at stake. A subject in such straits becomes not only obedient but potentially punitive of self and others. Fear then acquires a life of its own. It becomes its own object.[7]

Under the Uruguayan military's draconian and paranoid rule no meeting could take place without prior notification to the authorities and no organization could elect its officers unless the list of candidates had been approved. Even as late as 1980, the state's control of the right of assembly and the freedom of association took on Orwellian characteristics:

Deadline for Requests to Hold Public Events

> The Office of the Chief of Police of Montevideo, reiterating earlier communiqués and in accordance with the provisions in force, reminds those who are interested in holding public events, assemblies (of social, cultural, professional, sports, and cooperative institutions, businesses, mutual medical aid societies, etc., even in certain cases of religious organization, when they go beyond the mere exercise of worship on their own premises), elections, benefits, conferences, cultural and artistic events, tributes (to living or dead persons, to be held at sites, cemeteries, monuments, etc.), processions, including sports parades, scientific, technical and other con-

gresses, that they must obtain the necessary authorization from these Headquarters at least (10) days prior to the holding of the event.

It is advised that requests not presented by the specified deadline shall not be considered.

As for family gatherings, such as dances or other festivities, which, by their nature, bring together an unusual number of individuals, only the corresponding precinct must be advised.[8]

The military had, starting in June of 1976, changed the constitutional rules in Uruguay through a series of Institutional Acts. The first of these acts suspended the general elections called for under the constitution and scheduled for September of that year. Institutional Act No. 2 established a Council of the Nation that, composed of the Council of State and the Junta of Generals, was given the power to appoint the president as well as set general policy for the country. Institutional Act No. 3 provided that executive power would be exercised by the president, his ministers, and the COSENA. Institutional Act No. 4 stripped some 10,000 to 15,000 Uruguayans of their political rights. Included in this group were all individuals who had run for or held office in the previous two elections (1966 and 1971) and all persons tried for political crimes.

On the fourth anniversary of their rule, June 27, 1977, the military promulgated Institutional Act No. 7, which permitted the arbitrary dismissal of public employees. This decree, along with the loyalty classification scheme adopted by the regime, became a major instrument of control of the population and cornerstone of the national security state's attempt to purify the society by eliminating all "subversives" from public employment and threatening the livelihood of those who might deviate from the standards of the new society. Under Institutional Act No. 8, the independence of the judiciary was severely impaired; the Supreme Court was made subordinate to the executive, and the court system, in general, was deprived of its status as a coequal branch of government.

The human rights violations perpetrated by the military regime are a legacy with which the newly restored democratic government has yet to come to terms. This subject will concern us in detail later.

THE MILITARY'S ECONOMIC RECORD

Even when it comes to power by force, the ultimate test of any government, especially one in a developing country, is its economic performance.[9] When the military took power in Uruguay in 1973, they did so in the face of a decade and a half of economic stagnation, high inflation, and increased social unrest. Massive repression took care of the social unrest and any fears about the resurgence of a revolutionary movement. Economic policy and performance soon became the regime's litmus test, its ultimate claim to legitimacy and justification for its harsh rule.

After the armed forces closed parliament; destroyed the labor union movement; intervened in the university and secondary-school system; banned leftist political parties, movements, and publications; and held (in the mid-1970s) more political prisoners per capita than any other country in the world—thereby achieving totalitarian rule—they determined to alter economic policy dramatically. The long-term model sought by the military involved a profound change in the traditional roles of the public and private sectors and the response of the public sector to the influence of the external market. It was hoped that a free market economy would generate price relations that would maximize the use of resources and that state intervention would be limited to reducing barriers to effective competition. The external environment would indicate Uruguay's potentialities, helping to determine the price systems and thus promoting a healthier functioning of the domestic market. This liberalization and opening of the Uruguayan economy was basically a variation of neoliberal economic theory. It assumed a higher degree of concentration of production that would enhance the use of modern technology. Of course, foreign capital was considered necessary and compatible with this objective.

According to this neoliberal approach, Uruguay's decades-old economic stagnation had led to an absence of capital accumulation, which created a lack of investment and an economic environment that did not permit a decent return on capital. Money had therefore gone into speculative financial activities and/or was transferred out of the country as flight capital. The military and their civilian technocrats hoped to change all this. As we shall see, they failed miserably.

The principal architect of the program was a "monetarist" technocrat (*técnico*), Alejandro Végh Villegas, who had been trained at Harvard and received his practical experience as an advisor to the military governments in Brazil and Argentina in the 1960s. Végh served as minister of finance from 1974 to 1976, when he was replaced by his deputy, Valentín Arismendi, who served until late 1982. Végh wished to dismantle the protectionist structure of the Uruguayan economy, free the banking and financial communities from the restraints under which they operated, cut the budget, especially social spending, reduce employment in the patronage-riddled bureaucracy, and sell off most of Uruguay's state-run corporations. Végh succeeded somewhat in relation to budgetary and monetary issues and reduced some tariffs. He ran into opposition from some of the nationalist and populist military leaders when he advocated mass reductions in government employment and divestiture of such state-run industries as oil refining.

The military government's economic program represented a significant change from past policies. The inward-looking import-substitution development model that had dominated policy from the late 1940s until the early 1970s was scrapped in favor of an export-led model of economic growth. The results of this program and its cost tell us much about the ideology and interest of Uruguay's rulers. The model employed by the military was basically an attempt to reintegrate Uruguay into the world economy and reallocate domestic resources according to the efficiency of the marketplace.

The fight against inflation was Végh's highest priority. Uruguay had suffered through consumer price rises as high as 135 percent annually during the 1960s, and inflation had approached 100 percent in 1972, the year before the coup. Végh's strict monetary policy reduced these rates to the 40–67 percent level between 1975 and 1980. He managed this by strict control of the social service side of the budget and by a policy of depressed real wages. It is ironic that Végh might have had even more success in this matter had he not been up against a voracious military, heady with its preoccupation with national security. It has been reliably estimated that almost one-half of central government expenditures in 1976 were destined for the armed forces and police. Since then, such military expenditures have never been less than 40 percent of total expenditures.

The main thrust of development policy involved the liberalization of the economy, that is, the removal or reduction of artificial and differential exchange rates, banking controls, price controls, and tariffs. The model envisaged deregulation of finance and trade and a reduced role for the state in the economy. (The public sector in 1987 represents 19 percent of GDP and 20 percent of the work force.) In addition, inefficient domestic production was allowed to succumb to import competition. Reduction of the country's dependence on traditional exports—wool, hides, and beef—became a primary government objective and one that had some success in the late 1970s.

During this period, price controls on beef and several other food products were gradually reduced or eliminated, adding to the decline in purchasing power for the working class. All price controls were lifted by March 1979 with the exception of selected foodstuffs, pharmaceuticals, and some medical and educational services. An overvalued peso kept internal inflation down, as did tariff reductions, whose main function, however, was to help make the economy more competitive internationally.

The regime's policy had its most significant impact on the industrial sector. The goals were clear: to force hitherto protected industries to become more efficient or to go under and to stimulate the growth of export industries. The import-substitution industrialization model Uruguay had followed required enormous protective tariffs, especially in view of the small size of its domestic market, which prohibited the effective use of economy-of-scale production techniques. Végh and his team regarded these industries as inefficient, high-cost, and wasteful of resources. Phased reduction of tariffs and the elimination of credit mechanisms, such as artificial exchange rates (*recargos*), were instituted to let the strong survive and the weak die.

The government aggressively stimulated the growth of such industries as finished leather and textile products, which could compete in the international marketplace. The principle mechanism to stimulate these industries was a system of tax credits (*reintegros*) for nontraditional exports. These credits grew in volume to the point at which they represented 13 percent of the value of exports in 1975. However, they did produce the desired effect. The share of nontraditional exports in total trade rose from 25 percent in the 1972–1973 period to 64 percent in 1978 and was 48 percent in 1980–1981. The ensuing worldwide recession caused these percentages to drop significantly.

It is important to note, nonetheless, that traditional Uruguayan exports are not capital goods but rather finished apparel (leather jackets and wool sweaters, for example) based on agricultural products. In 1977, some 95 percent of exports were therefore based, directly or indirectly, on the agricultural sector, which continues to suffer from low productivity. In addition, as might have been expected, the 1981–1983 recession coupled with some protectionist measures, put in place under pressure of textile and leather interests in the United States and Europe, wreaked havoc with these exports, leaving these industries with high debts incurred under the expansionary climate of the 1975–1980 period and no longer recipients of the tax rebates granted until the end of 1982.

INDUSTRIAL AND EXCHANGE RATE POLICY

Perhaps the most controversial aspect of Uruguayan economic policy was the use of the foreign exchange rate. The quadrupling of petroleum prices in 1974 and the reduction of the international market for meat put new pressures on the government's economic team. Their response changed some traditional power relationships within the oligarchy. The cattle and sheep ranchers, whose political clout during the 1960s and 1970s was based on their role as generators of hard currency, saw their power eroded in the mid-1970s because of the regime's reliance on nontraditional exports and the influx of foreign capital. A preannounced schedule of exchange rate adjustments was made public by the

Central Bank of Uruguay on October 17, 1978, in a clear attempt to have a monetary policy that would correct the balance-of-payments problem and contain inflationary expectations through an exchange rate program and not through the traditional reliance on rediscount or open-market purchase of currency. This policy was quickly dubbed the *Tablita*, a shorthand for the exchange rate tables that investor and saver would now look to in order to plan their economic activities.

The short-term result of this policy—a change in relative prices and interest rates—coupled with an influx of capital from Argentina led to the economic boom of 1979 and 1980 when the GDP grew by 6.2 and 5.8 percent annually. But the Achilles heel of this growth was already manifesting itself in an increase in real interest rates just as inflation was subsiding dramatically. In 1979 inflation ran at 83 percent, but real interest rates were a negative 8.2 percent. In 1980 inflation was reduced to 42.8 percent, but real interest rates rose to 15.6 percent. The situation worsened in 1981, with an inflation rate of 29.4 percent but real interest rates of 23.5 percent; its most traumatic implications for a sinking economy occurred in 1982, when inflation was only 20.5 percent but real interest rates skyrocketed to 46.3 percent.

In past decades, the increase in the tertiary sector had been principally caused by an expansion of public sector employment and small commercial enterprises. During the dictatorship the increase in this sector was the result of growth in the financial sector and a strong upturn in the real estate industry, most especially in rental properties. The result of these tendencies was a further decrease in the participation of agriculture and livestock in the overall economy, declining from 19 percent of GDP in 1973 to only 7.4 percent in 1982. During the same period, banking and insurance increased from 3.9 to 6.2 percent of GDP, and rental housing as an economic activity increased from 3.1 to 11.6 percent. Negative real interest rates in 1979 meant that the influx of capital was converted into a construction boom and that the ability to sell goods and services at increased rates of profit was enhanced by the low cost of maintaining inventories.

Although the preannouncement of the exchange rate was the cornerstone of the stabilization effort, this instrument was part of an overall antiinflation program. Reducing import barriers and eliminating capital controls subjected the economy to greater international influences. "Increased foreign competition in the product market was perceived as a means of inhibiting domestic price increases, and greater availability of foreign capital was expected to reduce the real cost of credit to the private sector."[10] The progressively overvalued currency facilitated such foreign price competition, limiting the ability of domestic producers to raise prices in view of cheaper imports. Furthermore, it was recognized that fiscal and monetary restraint was necessary for the viability of the antiinflation program. The central government budget showed a surplus for 1979 and 1980 and only a slight deficit for 1981.

The stabilizing effects of preannouncing the exchange rate are most apparent, according to Mario Blejer and Donald Mathieson in an IMF Staff Paper, in inducing a substantial reduction in the public's expectations concerning future inflation:

> This is a crucial element because, when inflation has been sustained at a high level for long periods of time, institutional developments, such as excessive inventory holdings, fully indexed wage settlements, and high markups over original cost to reflect higher expected replacement costs, make achieving a reduction in inflation more difficult. In this context, a clear signal from the economic policymakers that definitive measures are being taken to reduce the rate of inflation can, by itself, have a significant impact on inflationary pressures. . . . The preannouncement of a gradual reduction in the rate of depreciation of the exchange rate may meet these conditions if it is taken as indicating a commitment on the part of the monetary authority to rates consistent with the announced policy.[11]

After 1974, import liberalization was designed to foster industrial efficiency and price competitiveness. According to the Ministry of Economy and Finance,

> The current import policy is aimed at improving the allocation of productive resources via an approximation of domestic to international relative prices, so as to guide investment towards those sectors in which competition abroad is more likely to succeed. The import policy also included other objectives considered necessary for a sustained level of growth. These consisted in obtaining modern equipment and machinery for the technologically obsolete industrial sector, in securing a regular supply of inputs, and in curbing the rate of inflation.[12]

In 1975, quantitative restrictions on imports, the system of prior deposits for imports, and all foreign exchange controls were eliminated. Import licensing, which had been used intermittently to reduce imports, remained only for statistical purposes. Most important, the maximum tariff rate had been gradually reduced from 300 percent in 1974 to 77 percent by 1981. The principal legislation to encourage foreign investment, especially for industry, was also promulgated in 1974.

The Industrial Promotion Act of 1974 was enacted to promote the establishment or expansion of industrial plants. Investment incentives and other measures are granted to projects declared to be in the national interest by the government. To be so declared, a project must support one or more of the following national objectives: (1) to reach maximum production and marketing efficiency based on adequate levels of size, technology, and quality; (2) to increase and diversify exports of industrial goods that incorporate the highest possible value added on the raw materials; (3) to locate new industries and expand or reform the existing ones, when this signifies more advantageous use of raw-material markets as well as available personnel; (4) to encourage selected technical research programs directed toward the economic use of heretofore unexploited national raw materials and toward the improvement of national products and the training of technicians and workers; and (5) to stimulate the tourism sector by means of the improvement and expansion of the nation's tourism infrastructure. Projects declared to be in the national interest may derive two major benefits under the Industrial Promotion Act. First, credit assistance is available through the Central Bank in the purchase of equipment, machinery, and domestic raw materials and for the modernization and/or expansion of existing industries. Second, import surcharges, import tariffs, consular fees, port charges, and other taxes on the import of equipment for the project may be waived.

A second major piece of legislation, the Foreign Investment Act, guaranteed the foreign investor the right to transfer capital and remit earnings on projects through a contract signed with the government. For the purpose of this act, a foreign company is one whose capital originating abroad constitutes more than 50 percent of its total capital. The act guarantees the remittance abroad of company profits corresponding to the contribution made by foreign capital. It guarantees the repatriation of invested capital after three years, except in the case in which special contracts with the government covering specific terms or benefits fix longer repatriation terms.

There is no personal income tax in Uruguay. Only net profits of industrial and commercial enterprises are subject to income tax. This tax is paid on the income of activities developed in Uruguay independent of the nationality and the residence of those taking part in the activities. The enterprise's net income is charged with a basic tax of 30 percent. There is also a value-added tax of 18 percent. Persons and businesses pay an annual tax of 4.5 percent on their property. The government can grant industries an additional deduction of up to 25 percent of property value when the investment is made outside of Montevideo. The farther this distance is from the capital city, the greater the deduction.

THE MODEL FAILS

In 1981, as the worldwide recession deepened, Uruguay found its export position deteriorating as external demand fell, the peso became increasingly overvalued, and protectionist measures increased in Europe, Latin America, and the United States. By the second half of 1981, Uruguay began to experience a severe recession. There were several reasons for this turn of events. Government policy was partly to blame, as were international conditions beyond the control of Uruguay's generals and their technocrats.

The worldwide recession that picked up steam in late 1981 had immediate repercussions in Uruguay. The gross domestic product was up only 1.3 percent that year after growing by 6.2 percent in 1979 and 5.8 percent in 1980—the so-called boom years. Growth turned negative in 1982, partly as a result of the deepening economic slump in Argentina amidst the political instability provoked by the Falklands/Malvinas fiasco. The only bright spot concerned inflation, which ran about 30 percent in 1981 and was further reduced in 1982. But this was nothing to exult about in view of the fact that the reduction in inflation was partly a product of the severe slowdown in the economy. The situation was getting so bad that the *técnicos* running the economy announced in March that they were going to cut government spending in order to restore public confidence and stem a massive capital flight drain of $165 million, or one-fifth of Uruguay's foreign reserves, during late 1981 and early 1982. To further balance the government's books, it was announced that major state-run enterprises—including fishing, the state airline (Pluna), and the Montevideo Gas Company—would be sold off if a buyer could be found. In spite of all the free-market rhetoric, however, the record would show that only a handful of public companies were denationalized under the dictatorship, the most significant of which was a bus company that was turned into a cooperative. There was nevertheless a serious weakening of the national banking structure as more and more local banks were bought or were merged into international banking institutions.

One of the most serious internal causes of the recession was the very high real interest rates that banks could charge under the deregulation put in place in 1978. Some results of these rates were a sharp drop in internal demand, especially for durable goods, a drop in capital investment, and a drop in inventories as the cost of money made it unwise to build up stocks of goods. Domestic producers were also being hurt by a free-trade policy that increased the availability and reduced the cost of imported goods. Sales of such domestically produced items as tires, electric appliances, automobiles, and apparel were particularly hurt.

These trends continued throughout 1982. However, the combination of the recession and the overvalued peso helped reduce inflation significantly from 83 percent in 1979 to only 20 percent in 1982.

But 1982 also registered the worst performance of the economy since the military took power in 1973. GDP fell almost 10 percent, with manufacturing down 17 percent, construction down 15 percent, and commercial activity down 23 percent. Unemployment rose dramatically during the same period, reaching over 13 percent by the end of the year and rising to over 17 percent of the work force by March 1983. The trade deficit narrowed in 1982, but this was caused by a sharp drop in imports that resulted from the severe recession in Uruguay rather than by an expansion of exports, which actually dropped to $883 million (from $1.2 billion the previous year).

The recession exacerbated Uruguay's debt burden, which grew rapidly after the quadrupling of oil prices by OPEC (Organization of Petroleum Exporting Countries) in 1974. A massive infusion of capital was required for Uruguay to make up for the huge balance-of-payments deficits that the oil price increases caused. Loans were easily extended by Western banks flush with petrodollars to an Uruguay backing the loans with gold reserves. Additional dollars were attracted from Brazil and Argentina by allowing Uruguayan banks to pay high interest rates with no taxes on these accounts.

Uruguay's foreign debt grew exponentially during this period—from $515 million in 1976 to $2.26 billion by April 1981. The profile of those who held Uruguay's debt also changed significantly during this time; increasing amounts were in the hands of the private money-center banks and holders of Uruguayan bonds, and lesser amounts were held by the international financial institutions or by foreign governments. Increasing by another 45 percent, the debt stood at just over $3 billion by the end of 1981 and rose to $4 billion by the end of 1982. It should be remembered that Uruguay has a population of under 3 million. On a per capita basis, Brazil's debt would have to be well over $160 billion to equal the debt burden faced by Uruguay's citizens. During 1982, the profile of the foreign debt changed as it expanded; public debt increased dramatically, whereas private debt decreased by some 9 percent (see Table 5.1).

Argentine real estate investment was the major source of foreign investment in 1980 and 1981. But as the political and, especially, the economic situation deteriorated in Argentina and its peso was devalued, such investment declined precipitously from $289 million in 1980 to $49 million in 1981 and only $10 million in 1982. The drying up of these investment funds coupled with the Uruguayan government's attempt to defend its overvalued peso led to a loss of some $570 million of Uruguayan reserves during the year.

On November 29, 1982, the Uruguayan government abandoned major components of its economic program. Reversing its three-year-

TABLE 5.1
Foreign Debt (billions of dollars)

	1981	1982
Public Sector	1.78	3.03
Private Sector	1.34	1.18
Total	3.1	4.2

Source: Banco Central del Uruguay.

old policy to use an overvalued peso to fight inflation, the peso was allowed to float freely, joining its Argentine and Chilean counterparts. The peso promptly sank from fourteen to thirty-four to the dollar. In addition, the following measures were announced:

1. Wages were raised by 15 percent as of January 1, 1983, to be followed by the freeing of wage negotiations to a type of collective-bargaining process.
2. Duties were eliminated for exports.
3. The long-standing plan to reduce all tariffs to a uniform 35 percent was abandoned in favor of a five-tiered plan ranging from a minimum of 10 percent to a maximum of 55 percent, depending on the degree of elaboration of the imported item, with the lowest rate for raw materials and the highest for finished goods. (The previous maximum had been 75 percent.)

When the peso collapsed, thousands of individuals and businesses who had invested on the basis of the preannounced mini-devaluations that were at the heart of the program found themselves wiped out in a matter of weeks or staving off bankruptcy in the courts. The government was not in any better shape. The central government deficit reached 8.7 percent of GDP by the end of 1982.

Pressed for funds and burdened with high interest rates and large loan repayments, the government sought to renegotiate its foreign debt. In April 1983 the economic team announced that it had renegotiated $711 million (some 90 percent) of its short-term debt and had received another $240 million in fresh loans. The government estimated that service on medium- and long-term debt during 1983 would take 25 percent of export earnings. Under the agreement, Uruguay would pay 10 percent of this amount as previously scheduled and the remaining 90 percent over six years with a two-year grace period at an interest rate of 2.25 percent above Libor (London Inter-Bank Offering Rate). The same banks also agreed to lend $240 million to the Central Bank at the same terms.

In addition, the regime negotiated a standby agreement with the IMF for $410 million. Under the terms of this agreement, Uruguay pledged to hold inflation to 40 percent and reduce its current accounts deficit from the more than 3 percent of GDP experienced in 1982 to 2 percent in 1983 and .75 percent in 1984. As wages and pensions represented 70 percent of the budget, restrictions on spending in these areas were required if the regime had any hope of living up to the agreement.

The government's decision to devalue in the face of massive reserve losses, in order to stimulate exports, held the risk of rekindling inflation. To no one's surprise, inflation was 20 percent for the first two months of 1983, matching the total rate for all of 1982.

The economic strategy employed by the regime sought a closer integration of Uruguay within the world economy, both in terms of creating a more attractive investment climate and in letting the forces of the marketplace rationalize the use of resources. Nontraditional exports were stimulated through state subsidies, and construction and financial services expanded, based on a fleeting but fortuitous economic and political situation in Brazil and, especially, Argentina. But the program resulted in failure. There was little direct foreign investment; few new jobs were created in the export sector; there was an exponential increase in the foreign debt and the dismantling of traditional industries producing for the local market.

The policy of stimulating those productive sectors that had natural competitive advantage, and thus increasing exports, had only marginal success. Exports as a percent of total demand in Uruguay went from 11.2 percent in the period prior to the dictatorship to 13.5 percent from 1974 to 1981. In 1982–1983 exports reached 15.8 percent of total demand, but this was caused by a sharp drop in total production and not to an increase in exports. The timing of Uruguay's generals could not have been worse. They continued to open Uruguay's small and fragile economy to world market forces just as a severe recession was moving the industrialized countries back to various forms of protectionism.

Exchange rate policy was at the heart of the government's antiinflation program. By keeping import prices low, it was thought, domestic producers would be forced to become more efficient and keep their prices down. The less efficient would not survive, but so be it. The Uruguayan government's decision to go with preannounced mini-devaluations starting in 1978 did help to curb inflation, but it also meant that by 1981 the peso had effectively appreciated some 29 percent in value. The result was a less competitive export sector at the same time that a worldwide recession continued to deepen. The fight against inflation and the economic liberalization required belt-tightening. Private consumption was reduced from 77 percent of GDP in 1973 to 63 percent in 1977, and real wages declined some 40 percent from 1971 to 1977. But the burden was not shared equally. During this period the employer's share of income went up 27 percent, whereas labor's share declined by 34 percent.

Social policy under the dictatorship was recently analyzed in regard to public housing and urban renewal by Lauren A. Benton. Her conclusions should come as no surprise to those who have seen and studied the effects on the poor of the recent military regimes in Latin America.

> The attempt to foster Montevideo's role as a regional financial center and the boom in investment (much of it foreign) in real estate and construction intensified pressures to redevelop the city center. The new situation contrasted markedly with that existing before 1973, when strict rent regulation had been an integral part of a postwar institutional setting designed to favor industrial capital and foster urban consumption. Low rents had depressed the reproduction costs for labor, had indirectly lowered wages, and had helped maintain a high average standard of living in a steadily declining economy. In contrast, the housing policies introduced after 1973 transferred the benefits of urban renewal largely to the fraction of capital represented by financial interests. These interests benefited directly by financing both public and private construction as well as indirectly through the greater specialization of the urban center in financial activities and other services. Changes in the central city directly reflected the attempt to replace the postwar economic model of agricultural exports and import-substituting industrialization with a new model of an "open" economy based on international banking and nontraditional exports.[13]

The military government's priorities are also evident in the shift in governmental spending. During the early 1960s, education took 21 percent of the budget. By 1981, education expenditures were only 13.5 percent of budget outlays. At the same time, security expenditures rose from 14 percent of the budget to over 40 percent in the 1970s and early 1980s. Domestic policy is only half the story, however. Uruguay is extremely vulnerable to the international environment. This has been amply demonstrated for events at the global level, but even much closer to home, events over which Uruguay has no control can wreak havoc with policy. The Falklands war as well as devaluation in Brazil and Argentina are examples of events on Uruguay's borders that can turn its economy from boom to bust (such as the effect the drying up of Argentine real estate investment had on construction in Punta Del Este).

The Brazilian, Argentine, and Chilean economic debacles share much in common with Uruguay's. As in Uruguay, Chile's decision to fix the peso exchange rate to the dollar backfired as the value of the dollar rose in world markets, thus exacerbating the effect on exports produced by the worldwide recession. The dependent nature of all the Southern Cone economies has been painfully exhibited in the 1980s. The crushing debt burdens, harsh austerity measures required by the IMF, and the growing social and political unrest that has accompanied them may be seen as challenges to the development models imposed on these societies by the military. The fact that many of the recently established civilian regimes are continuing many of these policies does not bode well for future stability.

The regime failed as miserably at development in human terms as it did in economic terms. Thousands of Uruguay's best professional, intellectual, and artistic minds went into exile, and many did not return. The university became a shambles, with little research of any technical merit or social relevance conducted. The Uruguayan regime certainly was successful at stifling political opposition, but it failed to provide substitute structures of participation and ultimately failed to revitalize the economy.

By late 1983 Alejandro Végh Villegas returned from an ambassadorship in the United States to once again become minister of economy. As the most important technocrat to serve the military regime, Végh had returned to help smooth out the expected transition to civilian rule. He publicly declared that his principal role was to see that the civilian government did not receive an economy that was a "garbage can." It is clear that he did not succeed in avoiding that result. The lack of success of the military's economic policies and their failure to achieve legitimacy or consensus led to a watering down of their own plan to reinstitute a civilian government under military tutelage; this plan was the final victim of the military's economic program, world economic conditions, and Uruguay's political culture.

LABOR POLICY

As was the case in military regimes in neighboring countries of the Southern Cone, the central aim of the military rulers in Uruguay had been to destroy the labor movement. The military government dealt severely with the traditional trade union movement. The National Federation of Workers was declared illegal in 1973, and all unions were banned until 1981. During the last quarter of 1982, the government approved a collective-bargaining law and associated legislation. At least on paper, some 180 unions were registered by the end of the year, but under restrictions that included no right to strike, no right to organize on an industry-wide basis, and limited ability to engage in political activities. The leadership of the banned unions continue to be prohibited from engaging in union activities. There were fewer than 30,000 union members in the private sector. Government workers were barely allowed to organize, although public employees were the largest group in the CNT, which at its peak in the late 1960s numbered some 250,000 workers. The aim was to atomize the labor movement by imposing unions at the factory level only. Federations were prohibited. Participation in electoral slates for union posts was limited to those workers approved by the Ministry of Labor—that is, to those who lacked any credentials as trade union or political militants.

Activists in the small, clandestine trade union resistance movement debated whether or not to participate in the process of reorganization called for by the regime's labor legislation. But before the debate could be resolved, assemblies took place in a series of factories. In four months, there were union elections in more than forty workplaces. The government tried to obstruct the unexpected participation of the rank and file, but the reorganization was already under way, and it proved difficult to halt it.

On May 1, 1983, forty-eight reorganized unions decided to commemorate International Workers' Day after ten years of silence. The work of coordinating this May Day rally gave birth to the Workers' Interunion Plenary (Plenario Intersindical de Trabajadores, PIT). The participation of 150,000 people in response to the union's call brought a sudden political turn, thus marking a new relationship of forces between the workers and the dictatorship.

In collaboration with the political parties, the PIT organized a series of rallies and civic protests including pot-banging demonstrations (*caceroladas*) and voluntary blackouts. This new stage of civic protest culminated in a rally against the dictatorship that brought 400,000 people together in the streets of Montevideo, the largest rally in the country's history.

The suppression of organized labor for almost a decade had helped lead to a serious deterioration of purchasing power. For the evolution of real wages since 1968, see Table 5.2.

THE DICTATORSHIP AND FREEDOM OF EXPRESSION

The policies of the military dictatorship regarding freedom of information and expression seriously disrupted the system of free public education created under the Batllista welfare state, created a void in artistic production, and resulted in a degree of cultural and informational

TABLE 5.2
Uruguay: Real Salary Index, Annual, 1968-1982 (1968 = 100)

Year	Country	Private Sector	Public Sector
1968	100.26	100.20	100.33
1969	111.47	111.22	111.74
1970	110.02	111.27	108.65
1971	115.67	116.03	115.28
1972	95.89	97.73	93.90
1973	94.29	95.56	92.92
1974	93.48	96.20	90.54
1975	85.22	87.73	82.48
1976	80.24	81.25	79.15
1977	70.68	70.81	70.53
1978	68.15	67.89	68.43
1979	62.62	61.77	63.54
1980	62.39	57.62	66.83
1981	67.05	62.44	72.01
1982	67.32	62.45	72.49

Source: República Oriental del Uruguay, Dirección General
de Estadística y Censos, Anuario Estadístico.

impoverishment for the population at large unparalleled in the nation's history.[14] Before the institution of repression, Uruguay had one of the most advanced school systems in Latin America. With freedom of expression and the autonomy of the system guaranteed by the constitution, primary, secondary, technical, and university education were characterized by a secular and modernizing approach to curriculum; by the application of rigorous academic criteria in teacher training and selection; and by a commitment of extending education to as broad a spectrum of society as possible.

In the early 1960s as much as 21 percent of the national budget was allocated for education, whereas military expenditures were 14 percent. By 1981, education expenditures were only 13.5 percent of the budget, and security expenditures consumed over 40 percent. Before the dictatorship, academic programs were updated periodically to incorporate all currents of contemporary thought; specialized institutes trained highly qualified teachers for the primary and secondary levels; academic posts were filled through open competitions; school attendance was compulsory through the first level of secondary school; the literacy rate in Uruguay was comparable to that of most industrialized countries; and the system of education with its markedly democratic ideology played a much more fundamental role than in most countries in the development of a sense of national identity.

At the national university—the University of the Republic—attention was paid increasingly to the provision and maintenance of research facilities, so that by 1965, research accounted for a fifth of the university budget and significant results had been obtained in such fields as medicine, agriculture, engineering, mathematics, economics, and sociology. High priority was given to the study from an indigenous perspective and to public discussion of problems relevant to national life.

According to the late former rector, Oscar Maggiolo, repression against the university dated from 1968, when the authorities felt it was a haven for subversives and began to withhold funds for research. By 1973, thanks to further attempts at economic strangulation involving budget cuts and delays in the delivery of allocated funds, the university had incurred a debt equivalent to a full year of its operating budget. Following a number of provocations and repressive attacks carried out by government troops and armed vigilante groups and the overwhelming victory in university elections of antidictatorial candidates, the government formally intervened in university affairs in September 1973. At that time, the Central University Council and councils of the various schools were placed under military control.

The government had intervened in the running of the rest of the school system in January of the same year, when the governing councils of the remaining sectors (primary, secondary, technical) had been placed under the control of a newly created National Education Council (CONAE; Consejo Nacional de Educacíon), whose members were appointed by the president of Uruguay on the basis of their political allegiance to the regime. The new curriculum for the training of teachers suggested that "equality is a dogma violating nature," and therefore both liberalism and Marxism are dangerous utopian positions, whereas the "realistic position" is founded on the acceptance of a society whose social structure reflects the "natural order of inequality." Presumably, this natural order could include nazism or fascism, as the syllabus describes both as "so-called Totalitarianisms."[15]

Intervention in the Uruguayan system of education was immediately followed by firings, forced resignations, and nonreappointments on a massive scale—estimated to have affected 70 to 90 percent of the university teaching staff, half of the faculty of the teacher-training schools, 40 to 50 percent of primary and secondary-school teachers, and almost all the primary and secondary-school inspectors. Many of those affiliated with the university (including two former rectors and six of the ten deans) left the country; hundreds were imprisoned (in 1981 the American Association of Atomic Scientists issued a list including 149 colleagues imprisoned in the sciences alone). Over 500 resignations and dozens of arrests at the university resulted when in 1974 the government began to require all those holding administrative or academic appointments in the school system to sign a "Declaration of Democratic Faith" swearing allegiance to the "republican democratic form of government" (that was how the dictatorship characterized itself) and stating that they did not and *had never* belonged to any proscribed organization. Because virtually all those affected had belonged to the outlawed trade unions and to the FEUU, they could choose only to lie about their past affiliations, and risk sanctions if investigated, or to refuse to sign and thus resign or be dismissed. As a result, standards declined in both teaching and research.

Already impeded as a matter of policy (since as early as 1968, the Uruguayan authorities had stated that the only research necessary was for development and that that could be obtained from the transnational corporations) and increasingly hindered by scarcity of resources, research practically ground to a halt in the years of government intervention in education—especially in mathematics and statistics, in engineering, and in the natural and social sciences; whole institutes and research facilities devoted to these disciplines disappeared. The exodus of so many of Uruguay's professionals, the widespread policy of political patronage, which determined appointments, and the authorities' pursuit of "ideological purity" also affected curriculum and academic programs.

In carrying out the academic policies consistent with their anti-democratic ideology, the authorities purged university libraries not only of works of Marxist content or sympathies but of complete collections of the prestigious Mexican publication *Cuadernos Americanos* and the highly regarded Uruguayan weekly *Marcha*. In the School of the Humanities and Social Sciences, all authors suspected of "countervening the natural order" were banned—including Antonio Machado (as the lyricist for Catalan protest singer Joan Manuel Serrat!), José Marti, and Jean-Paul Sartre, along with Marx, Engels, Hegel, and even Bertrand Russell (labeled a "Communist snob" by a government official). Psychology students were prevented from reading Pavlov ("for being Russian") and Freud ("for being repulsive and pornographic"). In art history courses for undergraduates, the use of slides was forbidden because the nude figures in Renaissance painting were deemed "offensive to morality."[16]

At the secondary-school level, textbooks and all printed matter felt to be or suspected of being "in conflict with the tenets of Western or Christian civilization" were submitted to the authorities for examination. Banned writers included Sartre, Kafka, and Machado, as well as all those—including Uruguayans—deemed "materialistic." In high-school philosophy courses, references to twentieth century philosophical trends were omitted in favor of topics such as "The Role of the Family" and "Communist Infiltration of Trade Unions." History teachers were encouraged not to cover the French Revolution in depth, but to stress such topics as the Spanish conquest, the Counter-Reformation, and the reign of Phillip II.

Before the onset of repression, cultural production in Uruguay was intense and of high quality. A wide range of opinions could be found in the press; foreign publications were readily available on the newsstands; the book publishing industry flourished, as did music, the plastic arts, theater, and film. Culture was available to the populace at affordable prices. All these facts of cultural life were adversely affected by the regressive economic policies of the regime and the continued exercise of censorship.

Censorship and economic hard times also affected the world of public events, with significant decline recorded in attendance at theaters, sports events, and especially movies. Many theaters and movie houses closed or fell into disrepair. Others, formerly occupied by independent theater groups, were taken over by the government for political reasons. Hit especially hard by the censors was the independent theater troupe El Galpón, which was based in Mexico after the imprisonment and torture of its members and the destruction and confiscation of its property forced it into exile. All those associated with El Galpón were banned from working in Uruguay; others banned included Uruguayan actress China Zorrilla, Argentine actress Inda Ledesma, and Uruguayan playwright Antonio Larreta. Also prohibited were adaptations of classic works that might imply critical attitudes toward Uruguayan society; this policy affected productions of Lope de Vega's *Fuenteovejuna*, Sophocles's *Antigone*, certain works by Berthold Brecht, and Tennessee Williams's *The Glass Menagerie*.

Numerous musicians were among the victims of repression, some because of their political views and others because of the content of their art. Classical musicians left the country in droves after being dismissed from the two national orchestras and sometimes prevented from working in the country; this was the case for Camerata Punta del Este, whose recordings were banned. Among musicians persecuted because of the political nature of their art were the *murgas*, brass bands that perform at Carnival and whose lyrics often contained critical commentary on current events. During the dictatorship they were prevented from using certain key words and referring to topics deemed sensitive; thus, in 1981, following the defeat of the military's constitutional project in a national plebiscite, all mention of the word "plebiscite" or reference to that event was forbidden; in 1982 the word *pueblo* could not be used, nor could mention be made of the cost of living.

A second and larger group targeted by the censors was made up of the principal creators of the Canción Nacional, a popular song movement that from 1969 to 1972 served as an important vehicle of opposition to the increasingly repressive regime. Most of these singers (for example, Daniel Viglietti, Alfredo Zitarrosa, Los Olimareños, a popular folk duo) were in exile, some after serving prison terms. Their records were banned in Uruguay. Broadcasts of the work of certain foreign performers, including Mercedes Sosa, Jorge Cafrune, Violeta Parra, and Joan Manuel Serrat, were similarly prohibited, and the routine denial of police authorizations for recitals made it impossible for any of these artists to perform in Uruguay.

It is estimated that Uruguay lost 10 percent of its population and some 20 percent of its economically active population in the decade from 1968 to 1979. By 1979, if overall one in ten Uruguayans had left the country, the number of academics, professionals, and artists who had left was much higher than one in ten. To see Uruguayan theater, one had to go to Mexico City or to Caracas. Uruguayan musicians were heard in Porto Alegre and in Amsterdam. The works of Uruguayan authors were published and sold in Madrid, Barcelona, Havana, and other Latin American capitals. Uruguay's best economists worked in Mexico City and in Paris, and Uruguayan academics held teaching and research appointments at the most prestigious universities of Europe and the Americas. This massive and unprecedented brain drain and the exodus of the majority of Uruguay's most distinguished artists deprived the country of experts and of much of its cultural life. The situation, of course, improved dramatically with the restoration of constitutional government. But many intellectuals and artists will not return, and over a decade has been lost in a rapidly changing cultural and scientific world environment. Those who did return found an impoverished and dispirited Uruguay.

6

The Transition Process

THE REGIME LOOKS TO THE FUTURE

If Uruguay's descent into dictatorship was slow and occurred in stages, much the same may be said of the return to constitutional government. In August 1977, Uruguay's military government announced its political *cronograma*, or timetable, for restoring the country to "limited democracy." The proposed plan called for a plebiscite in November 1980 on a draft constitution. The proposed constitution, drafted by the Commission on Political Affairs of the armed forces (COMASPO; Comisión de Asuntos Políticos) without consultation with political parties, their leaders, and the public, contained 239 articles and was not publicly released until twenty-nine days before the plebiscite.

The proposed constitution gave the armed forces direct responsibility "to take all measures needed for national security," which was defined to include the *"patrimonio Nacional en todos sus formas"* and thus would ensure the military's control over future civilian governments. Through the National Security Council (COSENA), the military commanders would share with an elected president broad authority to declare three different kinds of national emergency, including a "state of subversion," all of which would permit the suspension or restriction of constitutional guarantees and the arrest of "suspected subversives."

As the national legislature's authority to lift the state of emergency, provided for in the 1967 constitution, was drastically curtailed in the draft constitution, the document provided no effective legal safeguards against arbitrary arrest. The use of military courts to try civilians, prohibited by the 1967 constitution, was expressly mandated by the proposed charter for trials of subversive crimes. The draft constitution also made no provision for independent judicial review of military courts' procedures or decisions. Another provision would have converted the Institutional Acts and other extralegal measures decreed by the government since 1973 into constitutional law.

74

In effect, the new charter would have ratified all the illegal acts of the regime and established a legal justification for the bans, political dismissals, and abuses committed by the dictatorship. In addition, "national security," as defined by the military and incorporated into the draft constitution, would have given the armed forces virtual veto power over all future government action.

Thus, the text of this draft constitution reflected the fundamental elements of the institutional framework of national security as it had taken form from 1973 onwards in the various decrees and Institutional Acts: concentration of power in the hands of the executive; the direct presence of the armed forces in the key decision-making bodies; the limitation and control of parties, trade unions, and the freedom of association; the dismantling of the independence of the judiciary; and the extensive role given to the military courts. Individual rights would be restricted or suspended in the event of internal conflict, a state of subversion, or a state of war—the three states of emergency envisaged in the constitution. The proclamation of these emergencies would lie with the president of the Republic, subject to the agreement of COSENA, under the diminished control of parliament. Parliament was to be elected on the basis of a system guaranteeing a majority government through a mechanism by which the party with the relative majority would be assured 51 percent of the seats.

The constitutionalization of the National Security Council was to be the jewel in the crown of the perpetuation of military rule. The commanders in chief of the armed forces would serve as members of COSENA but, unlike cabinet ministers, could not be called before parliament. In case of a dispute between the president and COSENA, a Tribunal Constitucional would be established to resolve jurisdictional conflicts, including those involving political decisions. This body would be chosen, prior to the effective date of a new constitution, by the Council of State, the legislative body established under the dictatorship.

Among the transitional features of the military's constitution was an electoral plan that called for a single presidential candidate to be chosen by a "patriotic accord" prior to the elections in 1981. Subsequently, all relegalized parties would be allowed to have one candidate each for the 1986 presidential election.

Jorge Pacheco Areco, president from 1968 to 1972 and a hard-line conservative, counseled a "yes" vote on the military's proposed constitution as a way out of the de facto military regime. But he was the only major figure in the Colorado party to do so. The Blancos, led by exiled Wilson Ferreira Aldunate, were strongly opposed to the project, as was all of the Left. On November 30, 1980, as promised, the military submitted its constitutional project to a plebiscite. It expected to win and, in any event, warned the electorate that a negative vote would not change anything—the military would continue to rule. Unlike Chilean voters, who approved military rule by a large margin in a 1978 plebiscite, Uruguay's voters rejected the constitution by a 57–43 percent margin. As one observer of Uruguayan affairs later put it, "When the people rejected the plebiscite, four and a half years ago, that was the beginning of the end for the military. Fifty-seven percent of the population knew they weren't alone anymore."

The results conformed with the positions of party leaders. Some 85 percent of the eligible voters cast a ballot; the vote in Montevideo was 64 to 36 percent, whereas in the more conservative interior it was considerably closer, 52 to 48 percent. The proposal actually was approved in eight interior departments and was rejected in the remaining eleven. But the 42 percent of voters who supported the project included many who did not approve of continued military involvement, as permitted in the draft constitution, but who felt that any move toward the restoration of constitutional government was a step in the right direction.

THE PLEBISCITE'S AFTERMATH

The majority of citizens voted "no" on the proposed constitution, understanding very well that this rebuff of the military only meant a more difficult struggle to extricate the military from power. Hence the defeat of the military's project was a testament to Uruguay's democratic political culture and the power of civilian political leaders who, whether in jail, exile, or free to cautiously operate under the restrictions placed on them by the regime, had almost unanimously counseled a "no" vote on the plebiscite. The military had fought hard to sell the constitution and clearly had not expected to lose. When confronted with the vote, the generals claimed it was the constitution that had been rejected, not military rule.

Defeat in the plebiscite required a change in plans but would not result in a rapid transition to civilian rule. At first it looked like the military would try to ignore the results of the 1980 plebiscite. But soon a response became clear. Retired General Gregorio Alvarez, who had always harbored presidential ambitions, was made president in September 1981, and a new *cronograma* calling for the passage of a new law on political parties, the drafting of constitutional changes, and a limited election in November 1984 was announced by the military. Tentative and difficult negotiations were begun between the military and some political leaders. The specific timetable called for the remainder of 1981 to be devoted to the elaboration of a new law regulating the political parties; 1982 was to be a year for the reorganization of the traditional parties, including the election of party leaders; 1983 was to be a year for discussion and drafting of a constitution by the military and the new party leadership; an election and a plebiscite on a new constitution were to be held concurrently in November 1984; and, finally, the transmission of power was to take place in March of 1985.

Proscriptions were continued on such key leaders as Jorge Batlle, an important old-line Colorado politician and grandnephew of José Batlle, key leaders as Jorge Batlle, and the always-outspoken, exiled Blanco senator, Wilson Ferreira. The politicians had their own agenda, which included turning the internal party elections into another vote against the perpetuation of military rule, solidifying their own positions within their parties, and reestablishing the vigor and weight of the parties in the society.

THE PARTY SYSTEM

A spate of new publications were sparked by the mild decompression surrounding the 1980 plebiscite. The new weeklies were a breath of fresh air after several years of total censorship and the closing of several of Uruguay's leading newspapers and periodicals by the government starting in 1968. The first new weekly, *Opinar,* which appeared on November 6, 1980, had the greatest impact. It was run by Enrique Tarigo, a Colorado lawyer and journalist. Tarigo emerged quickly as a new political personality because of his impressive performance in a publicly televised debate on the constitutional plebiscite, during which he forcefully argued against its passage. *Opinar* enjoyed the support of Jorge Batlle and two of his lieutenants, Eduardo Paz García and Luis Hierro López. *Opinar* generally took a social democratic position, but one that was clearly within the Colorado fold. It would be closed frequently by the military government for its criticism of political and economic policy. Another, more centrist, Colorado weekly made its appearance in the middle of 1981—*Correo de los Viernes.* It was closely linked to the Colorado party activist Julio María Sanguinetti and was to become a cornerstone in his campaign for the presidential nomination within the party.

The Blancos also started a new periodical in 1981—*La Democracia.* Reflective of the party's mainstream opposition to the military government, *La Democracia* was run by the supporters of exiled senator and former presidential candidate Wilson Ferreira Aldunate. Because of its close identification with a figure, whom the military considered, even in exile, to be a major thorn in its side, this periodical was subject to repeated closures.

One new evening paper made its appearance in the fall of 1981. *Ultimas Noticias* struck a moderate tone. Its owner was Reverend Sun Yung Moon's Unification Church, which under the military bought one of the country's biggest publishing houses, Editorial Polo, a bank, and Montevideo's only luxury hotel, the Victoria Plaza.

During this period, the magazine that was essential reading for understanding government economic policy was *Búsqueda.* Closely tied to former Minister of Economy Alejandro Végh Villegas, it faithfully reflected the views of government technocrats and offered important clues to the future direction of policy. *Búsqueda* has become a very important weekly newspaper that reflects an independent center right political position and offers the reader the best available summary of the preceding week's events, along with detailed economic analysis.

On June 3, 1982, the Council of State approved a statute governing political parties that would regulate the internal party elections scheduled for November. The restricted nature of the military's restoration of political life was readily apparent. In the first place, the only legal parties were to be the Colorados and Blancos and a small right-wing Catholic group called the Unión Cívica. All parties that had been part of the Frente Amplio in the 1971 election continued to be banned. The individuals who were proscribed under Institutional Act No. 4, which of course included the leading figures of the traditional parties, would remain unrecognized.

The new law set the following guidelines for the selection of party leaders and for the national elections tentatively scheduled for November 1984: (1) Party leaders would be elected indirectly by 500 delegates elected on November 28 who would subsequently choose the fifteen members of the party directorate; (2) the traditional practice of accumulating votes by party faction was prohibited; (3) no more than two candidates for president would be permitted in each party. The intention was clearly to continue to proscribe the Left while doing away with the worst abuses of party fractionalization permitted under an unrestricted Ley de Lemas. It is interesting to note that even the restrictions imposed by this legislation were abandoned by the military before the November 1984 elections.

In addition, according to the new statute, no political party would be recognized if composed of individuals who belonged to organizations now declared illegal. The law also stated that "no political party will be recognized which follows the ends, ideology, principles, party name or type of actions that evidence indirect or direct connection with foreign political parties, institutions or organizations, or with another state." As General Julio C. Rapela, chairman of COMASPO, commented, Marxist parties would remain proscribed because Uruguay "cannot afford to put a worm into the apple which will eventually destroy it."

The military's hatred and possible fear of some of Uruguay's political class is apparent in Article 51 of the statute, which called for imprisonment of those individuals who during the political campaign "allude to or mention persons who have their citizenship, voting or political rights suspended, or that are being sought by the courts." This curious article was clearly an attempt to curtail the influence of the exiled Wilson Ferreira Aldunate and such figures as Carlos Julio Perreyra of the Blancos and Jorge Batlle of the Colorados. The government also continued to come down hard on public expressions of opposition to the tortuous and restricted road to democracy the military had embarked on. Opposition political newspapers and periodicals, including the Blanco *La Democracia* and the Colorado *Opinar*, were frequently closed or their editions confiscated as the internal party elections approached.

The November 1982 internal party elections, even more dramatically than the 1980 plebiscite, resulted in a disastrous political defeat for the military. Antimilitary candidates took some 91 percent of the Blanco vote and 72 percent of the Colorado vote. Together with a protest blank ballot of 7 percent, the opposition vote totaled 82 percent of all votes cast. The Blanco slate of candidates associated with Wilson Ferreira received about 75 percent of its party's vote.

This balloting had a lower than usual voter turnout for Uruguay, with only 60.5 percent of the eligible voters participating. This can be partly explained by the fact that voting in these elections was not obligatory, as was the 1980 plebiscite. In addition, the Left, which had an important stake and strong feelings about the plebiscite, felt less reason to participate in elections that only affected the traditional parties. In any event, the internal party elections showed a plurality for the Blancos, who received 53 percent of the vote to the Colorados 45 percent, thus establishing them and their exiled leader as the early favorite in a free election. (In fact, as we shall see, the 1984 elections would turn out far differently, with the Left able to run and Wilson still proscribed. The Colorados would receive 41 percent of the vote, the Blancos 35 percent, and the Frente 21 percent.)

These elections proved to be a major political defeat for the military, who still clung to their goal of a perpetual constitutionally legitimized voice in the direct exercise of executive power and restrictions on the Left. Building on the base of the plebiscite vote two years earlier, and attracting an electorate further estranged from the military by a rapidly deteriorating economic situation, civilian candidates identified as unalterably opposed to any future direct political role for the armed forces garnered more than 70 percent of the vote. The Blanco politicians, who ran on an even more antimilitary platform than the Colorados, received 619,000 votes to the Colorados' 527,000.

The big winner turned out to be Blanco leader Wilson Ferreira Aldunate, who dominated his party's results even though his name was forbidden to be published in Uruguay. His Por la Patria faction's alliance with Carlos Julio Perreyra of the Movimiento de Rocha easily captured over two-thirds of the party vote. In the Colorado party, the factions led by Julio María Sanguinetti and Enrique Tarigo proved dominant, but conservative ex-President Jorge Pacheco Areco's Unión Colorado Batllista did get some 28 percent of the party's vote. Of course the vote did not elect anyone to public office, but it was an indication of a massive repudiation of the military. It was also clear from the results that the Left, not being able to vote for any of their own factions or leaders, voted for Wilson's Por La Patria *sublema* of the Blanco party.

The military's initial reaction to its renewed rejection by the people was not encouraging. On December 17, General Yamandú Trinidad, minister of the interior, pointedly remarked that "in this country a timetable has been fixed and the Armed Forces are going to carry it out regardless of pressure or urgency from anyone." Presumably this included 82 percent of the citizenry. The commander of the army, General Boscan Hontou, a hard-liner, reminded everyone that the internal party elections were a first step and that the armed forces were still intent upon obtaining a constitution that would presumably include their pet project—a National Security Council dominated by the armed forces.

1983: LOOSENING THE GRIP

Wilson Ferreira's victory did not sit well with the military, who once again found themselves unable to engineer a *salida* (exit) on their own terms. Consequently, they again deliberately stalled any serious negotiations on a return to civilian rule, indicating through General Alvarez that there would be absolutely no change in the *cronograma*, which called for the drafting of a new constitution in 1983 and for a November 1984 election with formal transmission of authority on March 1, 1985. The military, taking advantage of the Southern Cone summer, did not begin negotiations with party representatives over a new constitution until the second quarter of the year. During June, Uruguay's armed forces celebrated their tenth anniversary in power. It soon became apparent that despite its latest rejection by the people, the military high command was still determined to impose a national security constitution on Uruguay and to continue to keep the Left—in all its manifestations—illegal.

During the first week of July, talks between the armed forces and the legalized opposition parties collapsed over national security issues. The military continued to insist that the security services should be able to hold suspects incommunicado for fifteen days as opposed to the forty-eight hours provided for in the 1967 constitution. The generals insisted on military trials for future cases of subversion and demanded a "state of subversion" constitutional clause that would expand the powers of the police and military far beyond those found in the emergency powers granted to them by the Medidas Prontas de Seguridad (Prompt Security Measures) found in the constitution. Enrique Tarigo of the Colorado party complained that the armed forces were preoccupied with subversion as they formulated a new constitution.

In early September, the military responded to the breakdown in negotiations by decreeing a ban on all political activity. By late October, General Julio Rapela, head of COMASPO, announced that the military, even without negotiations, would submit a new constitution to the people and hold to its promise of elections in November 1984. These elections would take place with continued restrictions on the Left and a ban on important individuals from the traditional parties. The civilian opposition vowed to oppose this caricature of democracy.

The Interpartidaria, as the coalition of the three legalized parties (Blancos, Colorados, and Unión Cívica) called themselves, now moved to a position of "civic action" against the regime. As occurred in Chile, demonstrations were organized around such activities as the honking of horns, banging of pots, and the turning off of lights at indicated times. Demonstrations occurred to coincide with national holidays: July 18, August 25, and September 25. On the last Sunday in November, traditionally election day in Uruguay, one of the largest demonstrations in the history of the country took place. Over 300,000 Uruguayans marched to demand a quick return to democracy. That same month, Amnesty International reported that some two dozen young people had been tortured after being involved in antigovernment demonstrations. Amnesty International also indicated that hundreds of political prisoners continued to languish in their cells. The year ended with further government repression. On December 30, riot troops and mounted police charged a group of demonstrations, beating many in the crowd and arresting over 100 people. The crowd had gathered in front of the home of the owner of a small radio station that had been closed after it broadcast the proceedings of the Blanco party convention. The demonstrators, as usual, had called for an end to military government.

On the labor front, the new (and still technically illegal) umbrella organization, the Workers' Interunion Plenary (PIT) supported the various demonstrations that took place, organized work stoppages, and demanded better salary adjustments than the government had granted; PIT also, of course, supported the right of workers to organize. As previously discussed, in apparent economic (and political) desperation, the government recalled one of its brightest civilian technocrats, Alejandro Végh Villegas, from his ambassadorship in Washington. Végh took his old job as head of the Ministry of Economy, where the armed forces hoped he could do something about the economic situation and rebuild some bridges to civilian sectors.

Also in 1983, an event took place that, although outside its borders, would have important political consequences for Uruguay. In fact, the election of Raúl Alfonsín of the Radical Civic Union party in Argentina had quick repercussions in Uruguay. Alfonsín lost no time in signaling his Uruguayan neighbors that he would like to see the restoration of democracy there. Many of Uruguay's civilian opposition leaders, including Wilson Ferreira, were invited to the inauguration of the Argentine president. When the principal Colorado newspaper, *El Día*, took the opportunity to interview Wilson, it was given a three-day suspension by the government. The atmosphere in Argentina, coupled with the increased isolation of the military in Uruguay, led many of Uruguay's exiles in Europe, Mexico, and elsewhere to plan a move to Buenos Aires with the expectation that they would be able to return to Montevideo before the end of 1984. As that year began, the military, although not budging from its public position, was meeting with civilian leaders, but at that point in time no one could be sure that the exiles would have their expectations fulfilled.

1984: YEAR OF DECISION

The new year finally brought an end to Uruguay's nearly twelve-year-old military dictatorship. The year started with continued demonstrations against a united and stubborn military; in August, an agreement permitted elections on November 25 and the installation of a civilian government on March 1, 1985.

The military chose to exit in the face of its increased isolation both domestically and internationally. The return to democracy in Argentina and the promise of the same in Brazil would have left Uruguay's military as the odd man out in the Rio de la Plata. At the same time, the generals were presiding over an economy that saw an unprecedented 18 percent drop in GDP from 1981 to 1983, with no recovery in sight. Their desire to turn power over to civilians was apparent, but there was one fly in the ointment—the possibility that Wilson Ferreira Aldunate would return and win the election.

In preparation for its exit, the military began to release important political figures who had been jailed for years. In March, General Liber Seregni, presidential candidate for the Frente Amplio in the 1971 elections, was released and permitted to represent his still-banned coalition. General Seregni had been first arrested in July 1973 for participating in demonstrations against the military takeover. He was released in November 1974 but was arrested once again on January 11, 1976, tortured for over one month, and not released until March 1984. Although prohibited from running for office, Seregni was permitted to lead his coalition in negotiations with his former peers and jailers in the armed forces. At about the same time, Luís Massera, world-renowned mathematician and a leader of the Communist party, was also released. In addition, the government began to allow the return of political exiles. In October, Enrique Rodríguez, a member of the Communist party's executive committee, returned after eleven years in exile, and on November 3, Rodney Arismendi, long-time secretary-general of the party, made a well-received return to Montevideo.

Once the military committed itself to an election timetable, it acted with a coherent strategy. Institutional Act No. 18, passed in the second quarter of 1984, relegalized the leftist parties with the exception of the Communists. This move was clearly made in an effort to get the Frente Amplio to support a negotiated exit for the military. In addition, the generals were well aware that the Blancos would not support an accord while Wilson was barred from running and that Colorado acceptance of a deal would not be enough to legitimize the process. The military also realized that if the Left were not allowed to participate in the election with its own candidates, it would probably cast its ballots in favor of Wilson Ferreira or his stand-in within the Blanco party and not for the Colorado candidate (which is what had occurred in the 1983 internal party elections, when the Left had still not been permitted legal party status). The military's strategy was well founded.

Even though officially banned, the Communists were allowed to run stand-in candidates under their own list (Democracia Avanzada) within the leftist coalition, with the understanding that the party would regain legal status under the new civilian government. The Communist party would support the pact between the armed forces and the Colorado party and the Frente Amplio, but would reject the Blanco party's position of refusing to negotiate while their leader, Wilson Ferreira Aldunate, was in jail.

As late as May 1984, the military was still insisting that a National Security Council with considerable autonomy from the chief executive be included in any arrangements for a return to civilian government and that military courts be allowed to try civilians charged with crimes of subversion. The armed forces also held fast to their proscriptions on the candidacies of Wilson Ferreira and General Liber Seregni as well as of the Communist party. On May 22, the legalized parties and the still-proscribed Frente Amplio agreed to resume the dialogue with the military that had been suspended the previous July. During the month, the Blanco party collected almost 600,000 signatures in a call for a plebiscite to annul Institutional Act No. 4, which barred thousands of individuals from political activity or from holding office. In response, the government issued Institutional Act No. 15, which abolished the right of citizens to call a plebiscite, reserving that right exclusively for the president. The political environment heated up further with the announcement by Wilson Ferreira that he would return to Uruguay on June 16.

The Blanco leader returned from his eleven-year exile on June 16 and, as expected, was promptly arrested by the military. Fifty thousand people turned out to greet him, and 300 were later jailed in protests demanding his release. A charismatic populist, he was feared by the military more for his personal popularity than for his policies. He was charged with insulting the armed forces and collaborating with subversives.

As Uruguayan social scientist Juan Rial has pointed out, Wilson Ferreira tried to pull off a *salida heróica*, a "17th of October," in which his return from exile would ignite the population into a mass demonstration that would force the military from power. He badly underestimated both the military's unwillingness to let him emerge as Uruguay's post-dictatorship leader and the capacity of Uruguay's citizenry to undertake a frontal assault on the dictatorship.

On June 27, 1984, the eleventh anniversary of the coup, Montevideo was turned into a ghost town by a general strike. The army, in a futile attempt to convey a sense of normalcy, ordered the buses to continue running. The empty buses did so with signs that said, "obligatory emergency service."

In late July, with Wilson still in a military jail and his party therefore abstaining from negotiations, the Colorado party and the Frente Amplio finally wrested an agreement on elections from the military. The politicians were strengthened by what had become a "national fervor" demanding elections. The agreement with the military was finally announced on August 3, 1984, at the Navy Club and is thus known as the Pacto de Club Naval. The dictatorship gave up its long-sought demand for a National Security Council, accepting instead an advisory body dominated by the president and his cabinet. A series of provisional measures guaranteed the armed forces the right, for one year, to choose future commanders and to monitor and react to "terrorist" activities.

These measures could be abolished or modified by parliament, acting as a constituent assembly during its first year in power.

The armed forces did not concede everything, however. Wilson remained jailed and banned from running for office. General Seregni was free to campaign for the Frente Amplio but was also prohibited from being a candidate.

Reaction to this early August agreement was as expected. The Colorado party and Frente Amplio negotiators saw it as the best deal that could be made with an undefeated and undivided military. Julio María Sanguinetti, former minister of industry and commerce in the late 1960s and minister of education in 1972–1973, the Colorados' principal presidential candidate, staunchly defended the agreement. "If there isn't an agreement, there are no elections. And if there aren't elections, what is there?" This was in keeping with earlier Colorado statements, such as an editorial in *Correo de los Viernes* in March 1983 that argued that "if we don't get a negotiated exit, we are going to be the lost generation of a lost country." Alberto Saenz de Zumarán, the Blancos' principal candidate and stand-in for the imprisoned Wilson Ferreira, pointedly indicated that, "these elections are not the elections we want." He promised that if the Blancos won they would ask parliament to call new elections within one year so that candidates such as Wilson could run. The commander of the army, General Hugo Medina, commented that the military could accept a Blanco victory as long as the party lived up to the agreement. "If not, we will see at the moment."

A Concertación Nacional Programática (CONAPRO; National Policy Accord) was established on August 21, 1984, in an effort to create a consensus among the parties and social forces on the various economic, political, and social problems with which a new civilian government would be faced. Although many detailed proposals would be developed, they were quickly discarded or ignored once the civilian government took power in March of 1985. The government of Colorado President Sanguinetti was unable to convince the Blancos or Frente Amplio to join the cabinet and therefore felt under no obligation to live by CONAPRO's recommendations. At the same time, the opposition parties saw the parliament, and not CONAPRO, as the natural arena for debate and the ironing out of differences. However, the effort of *concertación* served to unify civilians as they pushed the military back to the barracks. Typical is this Colorado party editorial:

> Concertación is not corporativism. Why? Because corporativism (or fascism or falangism) displaces the political power of popular sovereignty exercised through citizenship, with other corporate entities that gain title to that power. The citizen and his parties cease being the protagonists of

political life, decisive element of their purpose, their own identities become submerged in organizations based on specific professional interests. . . . When we speak of concertation, on the other hand, we are not talking about transferring the power of public political decisions from the parties, but procuring a mechanism for dialogue . . . a participatory opening, an exercise of civic life in the most harmonic form possible.[1]

These were brave and optimistic words, and CONAPRO *was* taken seriously during the months after the election and before the civilian government took power. However, once parliament was open and the Sanguinetti government in office, concertation was dead.

Juan Rial has said that concertation was an attempt at a political pact based on fear—the fear of a return to the military dictatorship that the country was only just beginning to move away from.[2] It was an agreement to have a democracy, but there was not agreement on economic policy or programs. Rial has remained skeptical. For him the question has become how long a consensus will endure when the government cannot deliver the economic growth that it was counting on to paper over the fundamental disagreements over economic policy; at what point will the "missing actor"—the armed forces—reenter the political game in an active manner. Assuring governability is the only goal Rial sees as the project of all the major civil forces in the society, and it is clear that he feels that will not be enough. We will turn to this dilemma in Chapter 7.

THE 1984 ELECTION

In order to understand the November 1984 elections and their implications for the future stability of Uruguay, we must be familiar with the peculiar electoral and party system that the country enjoys.

Uruguay's electoral laws, which were ultimately unaltered by the military, provide for a Senate and Chamber of Deputies elected by strict proportional representation. The president is elected by means of the "double simultaneous vote," which results in a concurrent primary and election. Basically, the election is conducted via a list system that allows several presidential candidates to run under the banner of the same party with the ballot counting for the candidate and his party at the same time. The candidate who receives the most votes from the party that receives the most votes gains the presidency. In the following example, the Colorado party wins the presidency by 100 votes to 95, and candidate A—the Colorado candidate with the most votes—becomes president, even though candidate D of the Blanco party received more votes (45) than did candidate A (40). Most important, this electoral

Colorado party		Blanco party	
candidate A:	40	candidate D:	45
candidate B:	30	candidate E:	30
candidate C:	30	candidate F:	20
Total	100	Total	95

system has been conducive to party factionalism and citizen identification with these factions rather than with the nation as a whole.

Under this system, the president, vice president, and departmental *intendentes* (governors) are elected by simple majority, but with votes accumulating within each party. (The 1830 constitution established a unitary government in which the territorial departments function as more than counties but less than states with their powers determined by the central government.) Again, the Senate and Chamber of Deputies are elected by proportional representation, with the voting lists constructed on the basis of the whole country as one geographic unit— that is, senators and deputies are not elected from a particular geographic area. There are thirty senators and ninety-nine representatives.

The use of the double simultaneous ballot goes back to 1910. The rules governing control of party *lemas*, or titles, date from 1934. The 1966 constitution required that a party be permanent—it must have contested and won office in the two previous elections—in order to accumulate votes. The political party statute of 1982 retained all of the legislation on elections and parties and added an additional caveat that allows factions to run under the party *lema* without permission of the directorate of the party.

This peculiar electoral system has resulted in a long succession of presidents who received a minority of the total vote cast (even if the president's party as a whole had received a plurality), and who therefore could not count on a majority in parliament (see Table 6.1). This system permitted splits in the traditional parties to exist, or even widen or multiply, without any loss for the Colorados and Blancos of their virtual monopoly of electoral results. Until the 1971 election, when the Frente Amplio managed to get 18 percent, the traditional parties had never received less than 88 percent of the vote.

As many observers have pointed out, the fact that the list system regards the whole country as one electoral unit has meant in practice that individuals put in the top few places on important party faction voting lists are guaranteed their Senate or deputy seats, in effect reducing electoral competition. In other words, candidate x does not run against candidate y head-to-head. As long as candidate x's faction does well,

TABLE 6.1
Percent of Total Vote Obtained by Successful
Presidential Candidates

Year	Candidate	Percent
1946	Berreta	27.7
1950	Martínez Trueba	19.6
1954	Batlle Berres	19.7
1958	Echegoyen	24.1
1962	Fernández Crespo	27.0
1966	Gestido	21.2
1971	Bordaberry	22.8
1984	Sanguinetti	31.2

Source: Rolando Franco, Democracia "a la Uruguaya" (Montevideo:
Editorial El Libro Libre, 1985), p. 155.

his position on the list guarantees him a legislative seat. Exacerbating
this situation is the fact that all elections take place simultaneously once
every five years. At that time, one voting list may include a party
faction's presidential, vice presidential, and legislative candidates, with
another list for the same faction containing the candidates for *intendente*
and the local legislature in each department (the Junta Departmental).

    This electoral system has always made it desirable, if not necessary,
for each of the traditional parties to offer at least two presidential
candidates in order to appeal to a wider spectrum of voters. The November
1984 elections were no exception. In addition to Sanguinetti, who is
clearly identified with the centrist to liberal wing of the Colorado party,
ex-President Jorge Pacheco Areco, a tough law-and-order candidate, was
the standard-bearer for the party's conservative wing. For those Blancos
not comfortable with the liberal and stridently antimilitary position of
Wilson Ferreira's surrogate, Dr. Zumarán, there were more traditional
Blanco candidates—Dardo Ortiz, or the more reactionary Juan Payssé.
The five factions that comprised the Frente Amplio agreed, as in 1971,
to field only one presidential candidate. He was Juan Crottogini, a
gynecologist who had been the Frente's vice-presidential candidate in
the last election.

    The elections themselves provided no great surprise. With General
Seregni prohibited from running and with Wilson Ferreira Aldunate
still in jail, the odds favored the Colorados. The Colorado party won,
with 41 percent of the vote. The Blanco party received 35 percent, and
the Frente Amplio, a relatively disappointing 21 percent—up some 2.9
percent, as compared with its 1971 totals. The 1984 elections gave the
Colorados thirteen Senate seats to eleven for the Blancos and six for
the Frente Amplio. In the lower house, the Colorados received forty-
one seats, the Blancos thirty-five, the Frente twenty-one, and the mi-

TABLE 6.2
Percentage Distribution of the Vote in Montevideo and the Interior

	Montevideo	Interior	Total
Partido Colorado	35.9	45.6	41.0
Partido Nacional (Blanco)	27.1	42.0	34.9
Frente Amplio	33.8	10.6	21.7
Unión Cívica	3.1	1.8	2.4

Source: Rolando Franco, Democracia "a la Uruguaya" (Montevideo: Editorial El Libro Libre, 1985), p. 165.

nuscule Unión Cívica party, two seats. Many observers were surprised by the Left's poor showing; they expected that after more than eleven years of brutal dictatorship and deteriorating economic conditions, and considering the significant numbers of first-time voters, the Left would do better. However, given the many exiled activists, prohibition on Seregni's candidacy, and the ban on known Communist candidates, the relatively poor showing could have been expected.

A major loser turned out to be the Blanco party and Wilson Ferreira Aldunate. In addition to losing the presidency and Montevideo, the Blancos lost in previous strongholds in the interior of the country, such as the department of Rocha. Adding insult to injury, the military finally released Wilson from jail on November 30, just five days after the election. Despite the defeat, Wilson and his son, Juan Raúl Ferreira, now a Blanco senator, believe that they have moved the party in a more progressive direction. Their block in the Senate and Chamber of Deputies, if added to the Frente's seats, could pose a problem for the future stability of Sanguinetti's policies and programs (see Table 6.2).

Because of the nearly twelve years of dictatorship, the parties did not have their network of local political clubs in full operation and thus could not rely on the traditional clientelistic politics they had historically used to obtain votes. This situation was exacerbated by the fact that the government bureaucracy and employment in the state corporations had been in the hands of the military for over a decade. This reality helped make television the key medium in the election for the first time in Uruguay's history. The televised debates between party leaders as well as between the candidates themselves became a nightly platform for analysis by the electorate and proved a springboard for the making of almost instant political careers, especially for some young Colorado politicians. Sanguinetti took the best advantage of this new phenomenon, making effective use of his own charismatic television persona and giving prominent exposure to some of the young men running for deputyships on Enrique Tarigo's List 85, most especially Opé Pasquet and Roberto Asiaín.

The election was a victory for the center. The president, Julio María Sanguinetti, a forty-eight-year-old lawyer with thirty years of experience in the Colorado party, entered parliament as a deputy at age twenty-six and was reelected in 1966 and 1971. He was minister of education and culture in 1972 but resigned in early 1973 in protest over the military's increasing political role. Sanguinetti is a moderate who makes excellent use of his oratorical and negotiating skills. He is very interested in culture and the arts and is the owner of one of the best private collections of paintings by Uruguayan artists.

A shrewd and pragmatic man, Sanguinetti orchestrated a campaign that justified a compromise with the military (no civilian trials for human rights abuses and no dismissals) as the best way to get the armed forces back to the barracks. His party has also shown a willingness to work with other political forces in the society in order to guarantee democracy's survival. In Sanguinetti's view, the *peaje*, or toll, that had to be paid to get elections was not very high. In his opinion Uruguay was dealing with a dictatorship that in the final analysis limited the vestiges of a de facto regime to three or four transitory measures that would either eventually be submitted to a plebiscite or, as actually transpired, would be allowed to quietly lapse after one year as provided for under the dispositions themselves.

As for the Blancos, there are several explanations for Wilson Ferreira's defeat. Certainly his inability to appear on the ticket did not help, although his supporters readily understood that a vote for the list headed by Alberto Zumarán was a vote for Wilson. Equally as important, Wilson Ferreira's continued incarceration deprived his party of an eloquent politician who would have made effective use of television. It must also be emphasized that many leftist voters had supported the Blancos in the 1982 party elections because the Blancos had been far more active in their denunciations of the dictatorship than the Colorados had been, but went back to the Frente Amplio, in the 1984 election.

Juan Raúl Ferreira was attacked in the Colorado press and frequently made himself an easy target. An editorial in the Colorado weekly, *Opinar*, chided him for his comments concerning the late Omar Torrijos of Panama. He had expressed admiration for the way General Torrijos had politicized his country—for example, calling on students to demonstrate and then sending in the police to break up the rally. *Opinar* implored its readers to vote for "serious and coherent people." Juan Raúl's temper did not help, and that, along with his youth and relationship with leftist groups and parties while in exile, made for an easy negative image in the opposition media. In addition, the uncompromising rhetoric of Wilson and his political lieutenants ultimately backfired by scaring away traditional Blanco voters. Wilson thought this would be offset by the young

TABLE 6.3
Uruguayan Election Results, 1954-1984 (percentages of total vote)

Party	1954	1958	1962	1966	1971	1984
Colorados	50.6	37.7	44.4	49.4	41.0	41.2
Blancos	35.2	49.1	46.6	40.4	40.2	35.0
Unión Cívica	--	--	--	--	0.5	2.4
Communists	2.2	2.6	3.5	5.7		
Socialists	3.2	3.5	2.3	0.9	18.3[a]	21.2
Christian Democrats	5.0	3.7	3.0	3.0		

[a]Frente Amplio running under the lema of the Christian Democratic party (PDC)

Source: Charles G. Gillespie, "Activists and Floating Voters: The Unheeded Lessons of Uruguay's 1982 Primaries," in Paul Drake and Eduardo Silva, eds., Elections and Democratization in Latin America, 1980-85 (La Jolla, Ca.: University of California/San Diego, 1986), p. 229.

leftist voters he might attract, but most of this group threw their support to the Frente Amplio.

Hurting Wilson Ferreira even more deeply was the lack of consistency in his campaign for president. His party first opposed the pact with the military because he was still in jail when the agreement was reached. But when the deal was done and the military stuck to their insistence that he remain in jail, the Blancos had no choice but to go to the elections lest they be frozen out of the political opening. They went to the polls but argued that the vote should produce a transitional government with unfettered elections taking place a year later. When it became obvious that the public, the politicians, and the military all wanted the election to produce a stable five-year government and not more political games, the Blancos abandoned this piece of electoral strategy. But all these flip-flops made the Colorado party look that much more stable.

The 1984 election was in many ways a replay of the last elections before the dictatorship, which had been held in 1971 (see Table 6.3). As in 1971, the Colorado party won the presidency, this time with a wider margin than before. The Frente Amplio finished a poor third, but given the repression suffered by the groups and individuals that make up the leftist coalition, their nearly 21 percent was considered a moral victory, even if this was less than a 3 percent improvement over 1971. And Wilson Ferreira saw his presidential hopes dashed.

But there were important differences in 1984. In the first place, the ideological polarization and radicalization so evident in the years prior to the 1971 election and subsequent to it was clearly absent. Second, right-wing factions of the two traditional parties were reduced to minority positions as a result of the process that led up to the exit by the military. This weakness on the Right was especially so for the

Blancos, whose right-wing presidential candidates received less than 10 percent of their party's votes.

Nevertheless, Sanguinetti, although running a generally dignified campaign, could not refrain from the occasional flourish of red-baiting:

> Behind that person who acts so calmly (Seregni) there are groups whose strength is well known. We have seen that the flag with the hammer and sickle which has been hidden for 20 years has started to appear. And there is no doubt that they are now determined to try to assert, within the Broad Front, their predominance in the working sectors. They are stating this. This is not a personal issue, it is a political fact. There is a philosophical battle, a battle of principles, regarding these ideas. A front which has totalitarian currents, to the detriment of those which are not totalitarian, undoubtedly represents a danger and a threat to the institutional stability of a country.[3]

Within the Frente Amplio, Hugo Batalla, who headed the Democratic Socialist faction started by Zelmar Michelini in 1971—List 99—received over 40 percent of the coalition's vote. Of the Colorados, Vice President Tarigo's List 85 actually received more votes than Sanginetti's own List 15, although Sanguinetti was the presidential candidate for both factions. Pacheco Areco's 28 percent of the Colorado vote undoubtedly helped the party to victory. For the Blanco party, Alberto Zumarán did exceptionally well, garnering over 80 percent of the party total. Senator Luis Lacalle's faction, the Consejo Nacional Herrerista, also did well and left Lacalle in a position to vie for the party leadership in the future.

The Frente proved itself once again to be a legitimate third political force in Montevideo, almost capturing the *intendencia*—in effect the mayoralty—of the capital, but failing by 15,000 votes. However, the Frente's poor showing outside of the capital left the coalition a poor third in the total vote—30 percent in Montevideo combined with only 10 percent of the vote in the interior gave the Frente its 21 percent of the national total.

7
The Challenge of Redemocratization

The November 1984 elections and the installation of a civilian president on March 1, 1985, returned Uruguay to the constitutional government for which it had been deservedly praised during much of the twentieth century. Sanguinetti surrounded himself with some first-rate ministers, most especially Ricardo Zerbino as minister of economy, Ricardo Pascale at the Central Bank, and Enrique Iglesias in the Foreign Ministry. Iglesias, an economist, was secretary-general of the UN Economic Commission for Latin America (ECLA) for a decade and is an immensely skilled diplomat with global economic and political contacts.

As it took office, the Colorado government faced three major tasks: reviving a moribund economy; dealing with the always conflict-ridden relationship between labor, entrepreneurs, and the government; and coming to grips with the legacy of human rights violations committed by the military dictatorship. In spite of the depressed economic situation inherited from the military, President Sanguinetti found several advantages in his situation. In the first place he does not have to worry about an electoral test of his administration, as elections for all offices in Uruguay take place concurrently once every five years. Thus Sanguinetti does not face the polls until November 1989. The Left's relatively poor showing in the party election gives Sanginetti the ability to reach agreement with the leadership of the Blanco party, most especially Wilson Ferreira, and be assured of a parliamentary majority on whatever measures or projects the parties agree to.

Uruguay's new civilian government inherited an economy that had contracted some 18 percent in the previous three years, a 13 percent unemployment rate, a 60 percent inflation rate, a crushing foreign debt, and an internal dollar-denominated debt that had brought new investment to a halt. Workers expected an improvement in wages, which had

93

The president of Uruguay, Julio María Sanguinetti, addressing the fortieth regular session of the United Nations General Assembly in September 1985 (UN photo 16577G/Yutaka Nagata).

dropped precipitously under the dictatorship, having fallen to 56 percent of their 1968 purchasing power by 1984.[1]

Dirty streets, broken sidewalks, uncollected garbage, frayed clothing, and rotting teeth are just some of the signs of the economic deterioration of Montevideo. Beggars, street gangs, increased robberies, and personal assaults are other indicators. The few nice shops in the downtown business district have elegant displays in their windows but no shoppers inside. In the still quite pleasant middle-class suburb of Pocitos, one can hear, late at night and early in the morning, the clip-clop of the horses and donkeys pulling the *carritos* loaded with scavenged garbage.

Professional salaries have collapsed. A senior professor's maximum salary at the university is $250 a month. The minimum wage is now $80 a month. The two and three-job route to maintaining a decent standard of living has become a necessity for the educated middle class. The old and the poor simply have no way to protect themselves.

The newly installed civilian government restored university autonomy. The deans of the various faculties and schools, all of whom had been removed by the military, were restored to their positions; the dozens of faculty who had been fired for political reasons were given their jobs back. The university returned to its system of tripartite governance, with each school electing a governing body made up of one-third students, one-third faculty, and one-third alumni.

The major problem that the university faces is lack of resources. Meager budgets mean that salaries are low, equipment cannot be purchased, and libraries have fallen badly out of date. The teaching hospital of the medical school—the Hospital de Clínicas—suffers from such a short supply of medicine and equipment that less than half of the operating rooms are in use. If Uruguay is going to have the skilled personnel to successfully enter the twenty-first century, something dramatic must be done to improve the technical and research capabilities of the university.

THE DEBT BURDEN

The government had inherited a broken economy. Its economic team had a herculean task that it set about accomplishing in a careful and calculated manner. They decided to concentrate first on renegotiating the massive foreign debt.

Uruguay's total foreign debt of $4.9 billion does not seem high in comparison to Brazil's or Mexico's $100 billion, but with a population of 2.9 million, the per capita burden is one of the highest in Latin America. However, on July 10, 1985, Central Bank President Ricardo Pascale and Finance Minister Ricardo Zerbino signed a new debt refinancing agreement with a committee of creditor banks headed by William Rhodes of Citibank. (Citibank, with $274 million in loans to Uruguay, is the major U.S. creditor, followed by Bank of America with loans of $167 million. The Banco do Brasil is Uruguay's third largest creditor at $151 million, and Manufacturers Hanover Trust is fourth at $112 million.) The restructuring involved $1.695 billion due between 1985 and 1990. The terms include a two-year grace period on principal and a twelve-year payout. Fresh funds consisting of new loans from thirty banks, cofinanced by the World Bank, will be dedicated to the upgrading of the country's hydroelectric system. A few days before this agreement was reached, Uruguay concluded a similar agreement with Brazil, under which $125 million was refinanced.

In addition to moving successfully on its external debt, the government has been able to alleviate the crushing burden on the economy caused by an estimated $1.6 billion in dollar-denominated internal debt. Originally, all of this debt consisted of private sector obligations; roughly half of it remains with the private sector. The government became involved when several banks had to be merged or bailed out because of nonperforming loans to the private sector.

The government reacted first by passing legislation allowing farmers and industrialists to refinance their obligations. About 20 percent of those eligible had availed themselves of the law's provisions by April of that year. In addition, the Central Bank, through a debt assumption and swap engineered for the Uruguayan subsidiaries of three Spanish and one Dutch bank, has taken responsibility for $263 million of bad loans that it will repay with ten-year, gold-backed treasury bonds. Both moves have gone a long way toward restoring investor confidence.

One of the major criticisms leveled at the dictatorship's economic policy has been that it permitted significant denationalization of the banking sector. Twenty-one of twenty-three banks in Uruguay are now foreign owned or foreign controlled. What makes this foreign domination more problematic is the high level of dollar-denominated internal private debt. This debt has been strangling the private sector, making savings and new investment virtually impossible. Foreign banks remain especially unsympathetic to the Uruguayan debtors and seek to repatriate as much capital as possible. As a result the "high bourgeoisie" are pretty low. There is no conspicuous consumption in today's Uruguay (with the exception of the Argentines in Punta del Este), and even the most strident leftists have been reduced to denouncing only one current enemy—finance capital, especially in its foreign incarnations.

One of the reasons for the significant increase in Uruguay's public foreign debt was the purchase by the Central Bank of troubled loan portfolios from failing private banks and their resale to foreign banks. During 1982–1983, the Central Bank of Uruguay bought up such portfolios totaling $500 million. Some $400 million was purchased under condition that the five banks involved be sold to foreign institutions interested in purchasing them.

In April of 1985 the Central Bank of Uruguay purchased $215 million of troubled private bank loan portfolios and received $325 million in new loans from the banks involved. The net effect was an increase of $540 million in public debt. It is estimated that public external debt was increased by over $1 billion by these maneuvers to keep the banking system solvent and protect some of Uruguay's largest private debtors. (See Table 7.1.)

As of mid-1986, total Latin American foreign debt was estimated to be $360 billion. The austerity measures put in place to service that debt, coupled with deterioration in the terms of trade, had reduced per capita income to 1976 levels, and in the case of Mexico and Peru, to levels of the early 1960s. The service on the debt would take $35 billion of Latin America's estimated $100 billion in exports. At the same time, capital flight from the region continued at a very high rate, and the estimated $100 billion that had been sent off-shore during the last decade

TABLE 7.1
External Debt (in millions of dollars)

Period	Annual average
1958–62	300
1963–67	459
1968–73	623
1974–80	1,360
1980–84	4,166

Source: Banco Central del Uruguay.

was not about to be repatriated. Knowledgeable observers have reported that Uruguay is a major haven for flight capital from Brazil and Argentina, with an estimated $1 billion in deposits from Argentina alone. However, these sources have indicated that these deposits are frequently transferred from foreign banks in Montevideo to the United States or Switzerland.

Morgan Guaranty Trust, in a major study on capital flight made public in mid-1986, has estimated that in just three years, between 1983 and 1985, some $30 billion left Latin America, including $7 billion from Brazil and $17 billion from Argentina. In addition, Morgan estimated that over $2 billion was sent out of Uruguay from 1979 to 1983, although there is no way to ascertain an exact figure. The Central Bank of Uruguay reported a $1.4 billion figure for capital flight from 1976 to 1985. If we accept the lower figure as a more realistic appraisal, it is still abundantly clear that Uruguay's capital flight represents a significant drain on resources and a major contribution to the increase in foreign debt. The repatriation of the bulk of these funds cannot realistically be expected, although there has been a cautious return of some hard currency during the first two years of the civilian government. These monies could, however, leave as quickly as they returned given Uruguay's free convertibility of currency.

Uruguay's continued negotiations with the IMF resulted in a Memorandum of Understanding covering the period from July 1985 through December 1986. Although entitling Uruguay to $201.6 million in standby funds, the IMF terms also called for a three-year grace period, a twelve-year payout, and an interest rate of 1⅜ percent above Libor. The interest-only period would thus last until mid-1988, and the lower-than-expected rate of interest would mean that payments during the first two years would range from $170 million to $186 million instead of the $250 million originally foreseen. According to the agreement,

Uruguay undertook to reduce its level of inflation to 60 percent for the mid-1985 to mid-1986 period and to 45 percent for all of 1986. However, inflation was 83 percent in 1985 and only dropped to 75 percent in 1986. Nonetheless, Uruguay did not miss its targets by an amount the IMF regarded as crucial.

The Uruguayan government also agreed to limit government expenditures to 18.75 percent of GDP, and the budget approved in early 1986 met this target. The government was looking for a 2–4 percent increase in GDP during the eighteen months of the program, and this target was met. The commitment to reduce the nonfinancial public deficit (including the Central Bank) to 6 percent of GDP in the year ending June 1986 and to 5 percent by the end of 1986 was also on the mark. For the IMF program year from July 1, 1985, to June 30, 1986, Uruguay was supposed to hold M1 to 60 percent and M2 to 51 percent. The figures came in at 78 percent for M1 and M2. The government ameliorated the potential harmful effects of not meeting the monetary targets by raising reserve requirements in the banking system. The IMF was not perturbed by the failure to meet the targets.

In 1985, GDP rose by .7 percent, with the bulk of the increase caused by a rise in agricultural production and an excellent tourist season. The banking system attracted some $200 million in new dollar deposits and the government raised an additional $200 million through the sale of dollar-denominated bonds.

For 1986, GDP was up over 4 percent. Exports grew by about 30 percent to over $1.1 billion thanks in large measure to the booming Brazilian economy. Unemployment fell from 13.5 percent in early 1985 to just over 10 percent by the end of 1986. The overall public sector deficit declined to 5 percent in 1986, down from 8 percent in 1985. The decline in interest rates and the precipitous decline in the price of oil in 1985 and 1986 gave Uruguay's economic team the breathing space it desperately needed. Investor confidence has improved, although this has not translated into significant investments in new agricultural or industrial operations.

The Sanguinetti government has clearly demonstrated its intention to play by the international economic rules. The maintenance of Uruguay's totally free convertibility of foreign currency by the new government is another indication of this position. The government's economic plan is clearly based on an export-led growth model. Although recognizing the need to improve the extremely depressed level of real wages, Uruguay's economic team remains convinced that only a significant improvement in exports will provide the capital and investor incentive necessary to make the economy grow. With this in mind, nineteen products have been identified and the fifty firms that generate 90 percent of Uruguay's exports have been targeted for special consideration by the government.

Foreign Minister Enrique Iglesias has traveled extensively to Europe, the Middle East, South Korea, and the People's Republic of China in a campaign to open up new markets. The government believes that if ten new markets can be developed that would generate $50 million each in sales, then export volume would grow 50 percent by 1991. The government is also aware of the importance of its bilateral trade with its Argentine and Brazilian neighbors. In 1984, 13 percent of Uruguay's exports went to Brazil and 9 percent to Argentina. The United States, which took some 17 percent of Uruguay's exports in 1984, was its largest trading partner. It therefore came as no surprise that President Sanguinetti pressed the issue of U.S. protectionism for textile and agricultural products during his state visit to the United States in June.

For a small export-oriented economy like Uruguay's, international economic conditions, trade practices, and commodity prices become crucial to economic well-being and future prospects. At the regional level, political and economic conditions in Brazil and Argentina exert a tremendous influence on the Uruguayan economy and polity. As we shall see later, the government is deeply aware of this reality.

POLITICAL SITUATION SINCE MID-1985

Sanguinetti's message on the first anniversary of his administration pointed with pride to the consolidation of democratic rule, the reduction in the fiscal deficit, and the resurgence of Uruguay in international politics. The assessment also included a realistic appraisal of the challenges the country faced and the need to modernize both values and structures if Uruguay was to enter the twenty-first century successfully.

> The long economic stagnation, the notorious technological backwardness, . . . an education that has not followed a world in scientific and technological revolution, a unionism highly impregnated with a vengeful spirit, a state that is barely rational, heavy and overburdened with its own functions, an entrepreneurial class not sufficiently prepared for the challenge of a competitive world, these impose on all of Uruguayan society the necessity for a vast collective effort.[2]

During 1986, the members of the Colorado party began a serious ideological discussion concerning the modern meaning of Batllismo and the nature of their party program. The principal focus of their discussions was the role of the state within the context of President Sanguinetti's desire to move the country into the future. Behind the philosophical debate was a struggle for future control of the party between Senator Jorge Batlle's List 15 (Unidad y Reforma) and Vice President Enrique Tarigo's List 85 (Libertad y Cambio). Each group has established a "think tank," whose principal function thus far has been the production of editorials and essays on the historic legacy of José Batlle and the need for state administrative reform.

It appears that Batlle's faction is intent on dressing up the classic Batllista ideology, whereas the "young Turks" around Tarigo, such as Opé Pasquet and Roberto Asiaín, are looking for a new vocabulary that would fit their more technocratic outlook. At the same time, Senator Manuel Flores Silva of the Corriente Batllista Independiente (CBI; List 89) started a magazine called *Reflexiones del Batllismo*, which purported to be a partywide platform for ideological discussion, but which could clearly also serve to solidify his position as the leader of the social democratic faction of the Colorado party.

Flores Silva staked out a position on the left portion of the party spectrum during the 1984 election campaign, but since then has increased his attacks on the Marxist Left, blaming them for "ideological barriers" that prevent the modernization of civil society and its relationship to the state. He sees Uruguayan society as caught in an almost oedipal relationship with the state, which is reinforced by the classic Uruguayan dichotomies of country–city, worker–owner, and university–political power and by the corporativist practices of both the Right and the Left. Ideologically, he believes that the sterile and dogmatic vocabulary of Marxism-Leninism must be superseded by a political liberalism based on the individual and social democracy.

THE POLITICAL ECONOMY

The Uruguayan state may be considered a bloated, interventionist welfare machine, but curiously its impact on some sectors of the economy is quite limited. For instance, Uruguay's government devotes only 1.4 percent of its expenditures to agriculture, compared with 6.1 percent in Mexico, 6.3 percent in Brazil, and 2.1 percent in the United States. On the other hand, 4 percent of GDP is dedicated to defense spending compared with .9 percent in Brazil, .5 percent in Mexico, and 5.2 percent in the United States. That tiny Uruguay should devote so much of its scarce resources to its military is a legacy of twelve years of dictatorship and not of welfare-state ideology.

In 1969 total public employment in Uruguay was 213,000. By the end of 1985 it had reached 241,000, but almost all of the increase is accounted for by additions in military and police personnel. In terms of central government positions—that is, excluding employment in the *entes autónomos*—the Defense and Interior ministries accounted for 40 percent of all positions (almost 43,000 and over 26,000 posts, respectively). National security, and not the welfare state, is responsible for the growth of this public sector in the last seventeen years.

According to IMF data for 1982, government income as a percentage of GDP was 24 percent in Uruguay, compared to 32 percent in Brazil, 20 percent in Mexico, and 35 percent in the United States. Taxes equalled 23 percent of GDP in Uruguay as against 25 percent in Brazil, 18 percent in Mexico, and 29 percent in the United States. Uruguay's major state-owned industrial corporation, ANCAP, which is responsible for petroleum refining and the production of alcohol and cement, accounted for 4 percent of GDP. As the dictatorship came to an end, the expansion of government expenditure was the result, in large measure, of the purchase of nonperforming loans from desperate private banks by Uruguay's Central Bank. All this does not mean to suggest that the Uruguayan state does not have a major influence on the economy. It employs 20 percent of the work force and is responsible for an equal proportion of GDP. More important, everyone from labor to retired persons (over 300,000 people) to the political class itself looks to the Uruguayan state for protection and sustenance.

In certain areas, Uruguay has remained steadfastly committed to the free-market model. Uruguay is the only country on the continent that permits the free buying and selling of foreign currencies. In addition, banks constantly advertise their interest rates for dollar deposits, and the government raises hard currency by issuing gold-backed treasury bonds denominated in dollars. For such reasons, Uruguay has once again been dubbed the "Switzerland of South America." The title used to refer to its constitutional stability and the civil liberties enjoyed by the population. It now confirms Uruguay's role as a haven for foreign capital. As I mentioned earlier, in recent years significant flight capital has been deposited in the branches of international banks located in Montevideo. Most of this money is usually from Brazil and Argentina, but when a Socialist government was elected in Spain, an estimated $3 billion poured into Uruguayan bank accounts. The twenty-three banks in the country, only two of which are purely Uruguayan, are not there just for the business provided by the relatively small number of multinationals that do business in Uruguay. The small domestic economy has not attracted these banks. Rather, it is their ability to capture the funds represented by capital flight, even if these funds are quickly transferred to Switzerland or the United States, that has motivated their banking presence in Montevideo.

One can walk into the branch of a foreign bank in Montevideo with $10 million in cash, ask for it to be deposited into an account elsewhere in the world, and no questions will be asked. None of this changed when the military handed power over to the Sanguinetti government. In fact, the government's willingness to save troubled banks by buying up their nonperforming loan portfolios, as well as the 2.6 million ounces of gold Uruguay accumulated during its prosperous years, gives the depositor a sense of security.

GOVERNMENT AND THE UNIONS

The most important consideration in understanding the relationship of labor to government in Uruguay is that the two traditional parties, Blanco and Colorado, have never had strong ties to labor. The Left, on the other hand, and most especially the Communist party, has traditionally controlled the labor union movement. With the political opening that took place at the end of 1984, the Blancos and some social democratic elements within the Frente Amplio obtained some leadership positions within organized labor. However, the competition between old-line Communist labor leaders, new anarchist activists, and leaders from more traditional party sectors made it difficult for the newly installed Colorado government to find a cohesive union leadership with whom it could make a deal in order to establish labor peace. The government was confronted by the usual dilemma in Uruguay: The traditional parties gained electoral power in the November 1984 election and with it control of state corporations and the bureaucracy; however, as usual, labor and other social organizations and movements were in the hands of the Left.

After he assumed office, President Sanguinetti sought an agreement among entrepreneurs, labor, and the opposition parties similar to what Felipe Gonzalez had achieved in Spain through the Moncloa Pact, which helped establish labor peace in Spain. Such an agreement proved elusive partly because of the internal divisions in the labor movement. The Communist party faced strong competition for its control of the union movement. The return of democracy brought with it a vigorous renewal of union activity. The new union confederation that had emerged toward the end of the dictatorship—the Plenario Intersindical de Trabajadores (PIT)—merged with the old Communist-dominated CNT into a general federation known by its anagram, PIT-CNT. Internal elections took place in dozens of unions with the Communists gaining a majority of union delegates, but receiving strong competition from a coalition of social democratic, Socialist, and Christian Democratic union leaders. Indeed, several key unions, including those involving bank and health workers, elected non-Communist leaders.

There were numerous strikes and work stoppages during 1985 and 1986. However, the government reacted with maturity and firmness in regard to labor unrest by recognizing that after twelve years of banned union activity and a 40 percent decline in real wages, Uruguay's workers need to vent their frustrations and assuage their hunger. The government is fully conscious of the labor picture in Uruguay. Some 230,000 of Uruguay's 1.1 million economically active population are unionized. There were some 150,000 unemployed persons in Uruguay during 1985. The economy must provide jobs for 50,000 new workers that will enter the labor market in each of the next three years, beginning with 1987, just to keep the unemployment rate at its current figure of 11–12 percent.

President Sanguinetti faced his first general strike on October 4, 1985, when the PIT-CNT struck in sympathy with workers on the state-owned railroad who had been locked in a bitter dispute with the government for weeks. With unemployment still running close to 12 percent and a struggle for control of the central labor confederation between Communist and non-Communist political factions, one union after another went on strike for better pay or job security. At the same time, the government has made it clear, in word and in deed, that it will not tolerate worker sit-ins at factories, schools, or other public buildings. The conflictual labor situation was of concern to the business community and to the government, which employs 20 percent of the work force. President Sanguinetti and his minister of labor, Hugo Fernández Faingold, have devoted enormous time and energy in an effort to reduce labor unrest.

The PIT-CNT held a national convention in early December during which a significant split developed. The non-Communist delegates, representing some 40 percent of the congress, walked out in protest over Communist manipulation of the agenda for the meeting and Communist attempts to dominate key positions in the labor federation. This split has had immediate repercussions in the Frente Amplio, as the parties in the Frente are obviously the same ones that are contesting representation and leadership roles within the labor movement.

Relations between the government and labor worsened in mid-1986. The legislation codifying union rights was caught between conservative entrepreneurs, a skeptical union movement, and a divided parliament. The project on union rights that came out of a legislative commission in mid-1986 was harshly criticized by entrepreneurs, supported by union leaders, and provoked a split among the politicians. Luis Brezzo, deputy minister of labor, surprised many observers by coming out against the project even though his boss, Labor Minister Fernández Faingold, supported it. If the bill passed, it would be the first legislation in Uruguay defining union rights and protecting the activities of union activists. However, as such activities are virtually unchecked and union rights have been sacrosanct by custom and usage for decades (except of course during the dictatorship), some radical union leaders see any legislation on labor as an attempt to regulate their activities. Employers were upset by the fact that the proposed bill said nothing about worker responsibilities and obligations.

Tensions were further exacerbated by a government announcement that in the future it might declare certain public offices and activities "essential services" and thus prevent strikes or work stoppages in such areas as public health, pension administration, and port facilities. The announcement was met with hostility by the labor movement. Leaders of the PIT-CNT denounced the move as the beginning of the Colorado government's attempt to limit the right to strike and the first step in a plan to regulate union activities. The PIT-CNT called a general strike for June 17, the day President Sanguinetti would be received in Washington by President Reagan during his official state visit to the United States.

President Sanguinetti had exacerbated government-labor relations in early June by declaring:

> There is also an old style that is dying in union life and another that is being born. The old style that is dying is the unionism of anger and resentment that only knows how to paralyze in order to demonstrate that it still has strength. This syndicalism that is dying is going to give way to a new syndicalism which defends the worker through better productivity and thus gives stability to employees and the enterprise.[2]

In July the executive committee of the PIT-CNT announced that the extraordinary convention that was scheduled for 1986 would not take place until May 1987. The decision was bitterly attacked by the Blancos, who had made some inroads into several local unions and saw the decision as a deliberate attempt by the Communist labor leaders to hold on to control of the executive board without having to test their actual strength in the delegate elections that would precede the congress. There is much merit to their argument in view of the fact that the last congress broke up when almost half the delegates walked out in protest over attempts by the Communists to stack the executive committee.

HUMAN RIGHTS: THE MILITARY AND DEMOCRACY

As I previously described, human rights were systematically and grossly violated by the military dictatorship. Partly in acknowledgement of this reality, the Colorado government moved quickly to release all remaining prisoners, including the top leadership of the Tupamaros. These individuals had received unusually harsh and barbaric treatment during their years in captivity. In March 1985 the Uruguayan parliament passed a compromise amnesty law acceptable to President Sanguinetti, who was opposed to a blanket amnesty, which would have included those individuals convicted of so-called blood crimes—assassination and kidnapping. The law provided for general amnesty for about 210 prisoners and a civilian court review and subsequent commutation of sentence for some 62 other prisoners, including the founder of the Tupamaros, Raúl Sendic. By the third week of March, all political prisoners had been released.

The release of guerrillas who had participated in kidnappings and murder remains for President Sanguinetti an act of national pacification ("a homage to peace") and not an act of forgiveness or exoneration. Sanguinetti believes that national pacification also requires an amnesty for the military and its actions during the dictatorship. He sees the military dictatorship that Uruguay was subjected to from 1973 to 1984 as the direct result of guerrilla activity, which caused the military to depart from its traditional apolitical role. For these and other reasons, he has argued that because of the passage of time and the relatively small number of cases of people who disappeared in Uruguay—27 (although the number rises to over 150 if those Uruguayans who disappeared in Argentina are included)—the Uruguayan experience is qualitatively different from that of Argentina. Essentially, Sanguinetti believes that there was no conscious decision to physically eliminate human beings in Uruguay, whereas in Argentina the evidence does point to such a concrete decision by that country's armed forces.

Nevertheless, the issue of torture, rape, kidnap, and disappearances has remained unresolved. In Uruguay, a private professional association was the first institution to investigate its members for human rights violations. The Uruguayan Medical Union (SMU; Sindicato Médico del Uruguay) created an ethics commission prior to the 1984 elections to investigate the role of physicians in cases of torture. This organization can take action against a doctor even if he has not been found guilty in court. By the end of 1985, proceedings had been initiated against sixty individuals.

In May 1986, an International Seminar on Torture took place in Uruguay that looked into the psychological effects of torture, international norms on human rights abuses, the responsibility of the medical profession, and the doctrine of national security as it relates to torture. The symposium's chief sponsor was the SMU, which continued to be the only institution in Uruguay willing to look into the subject of human rights abuses and judge some of its own members. However, a church-related human rights group, Servicio Paz y Justicia (SERPAJ), headed by Rev. Luis Pérez Aguirre, emerged during the dictatorship and publicly took up the cause of human rights violations and the victims of such violations. SERPAJ continues to be outspoken on the human rights legacy of the dictatorship.

Maxwell G. Bloche of the Yale Law School stated in a 1986 article in the Journal of the American Medical Association that some doctors "played a significant role" in the illegal detentions and tortures that took place under the dictatorship and "systematically served the bureaucracy of state terror" in Uruguay.[4] After interviewing more than forty doctors, prisoners, politicians, and military personnel, Dr. Bloche concluded that torture was routine and that doctors examined prisoners, provided confidential information to their jailers, and made determinations as to whether torture sessions could continue. As of mid-1986, only one person—Dr. Eduardo Díaz—had been dismissed from his public health job by the Sanguinetti government. He was charged with having falsified an autopsy report on the death of a prisoner.

Three human rights cases have most captured public consciousness, including the consciences of government politicians: the June 1976 kidnapping and murders of Frente Senator Zelmar Michelini and Blanco Deputy Héctor Gutiérrez Ruiz in Buenos Aires; the poisoning of Cecilia Fontana de Heber, wife of legislator Mario Heber, a conservative but antimilitary Blanco senator; and the forced removal from the Venezuelan embassy in Montevideo, and subsequent disappearance, of Elena Quinteros. The Venezuelan government broke diplomatic relations with Uruguay's military government over this incident.

The investigation of the Michelini and Gutiérrez Ruiz killings has continued to prove particularly sensitive. In a letter to Carlos Quijano, editor of *Marcha*, dated May 12, 1976, Michelini discussed his meeting in Buenos Aires with Alejandro Végh Villegas, the Uruguayan regime's finance minister and political advisor. Six days later, Michelini was kidnapped, tortured, and killed, destroying any possibility of a negotiated *apertura*.

Although there have been no official indictments in these cases, it is general knowledge in Montevideo that Manuel Cordero, currently a lieutenant colonel in the Uruguayan army, accompanied Pedro Mattos, currently a captain, to Buenos Aires and paid him $12,000 to kill the two Uruguayan politicians. The entire episode was designated "Operation Condor" by the Uruguayan armed forces. In Argentina, a human rights organization, the Centro de Estudios Legales y Sociales (CELS), asked for the detention of nine Argentine and three Uruguayan military personnel in the death of Héctor Gutiérrez Ruiz and Zelmar Michelini. The Uruguayans named were José Nino Gavazzo and Cordero and Mattos.

The legislative commission investigating the assassinations was shocked to find that its supposedly secret testimony was leaked to the conservative Uruguayan daily *El País*. Tension between the legislative and executive branches over the entire matter was exacerbated when Defense Minister Juan Vicente Chiarino announced that he had forwarded all of the commission's documents and proceedings to the military justice division of the army.

As originally floated to test public opinion, the Colorado party's amnesty project would have forgiven all crimes committed by the armed forces and police in the period beginning with the declaration of a state of internal war in April 1972 and ending with the transmission of power to a civilian government in March 1985. Homicide trials would have been conducted under military court jurisdiction with the right of appeal to the civilian Supreme Court of Justice. This proposal was met with broadly negative reactions from both the Blancos and the Left. In addition, noted jurists from all three parties felt the proposal was constitutionally weak. To complicate matters even further, hard-liners in the armed forces continued to insist that they would not be a party to any attempts to judge their actions, including an amnesty!

According to a special study carried out by the independent newsweekly *Búsqueda*, some 350 Uruguayans died in the violence in the Southern Cone during the 1960s and 1970s.[5] The figures include 49 Tupamaros and 50 armed forces and police personnel that were killed in armed confrontations; 73 prisoners who died while incarcerated; 33 others who died under "other circumstances" in Uruguay and 16 who died similarly in Argentina. In addition, 110 Uruguayans disappeared in Argentina, 25 in Uruguay, and 2 in Paraguay.

In a poll taken by Uruguay's most respected polling organization, Equipos Consultores, in June 1986, some 85 percent of the respondents indicated that the military had committed human rights violations during the dictatorship and 70 percent expressed the opinion that those who committed such violations should be punished. Only 10 percent, however, thought there would be a resolution of the question during 1986; 27 percent thought it would take longer. Some 40 percent expressed the opinion that no one would ever be punished for the human rights abuses that had been committed.

The armed forces did not go back to the barracks without sending some clear signals concerning their future role in politics and the defense of their interests. The army commander, Lieutenant General Hugo Medina, indicated just a few weeks before the Sanguinetti inauguration that "if we are obliged, we will have no choice but to carry out another coup d'état." A few weeks before he stepped down as president, General Gregorio Alvarez signed a decree ordering the destruction of "documents without historic interest" in the Ministries of Defense and Interior. This was a public admission of the military dictatorship's intention to eliminate all evidence that could be used in congressional investigations or civil trials of human rights abuses. Sanguinetti thus faces a military high command that remains intact, does not intend to pay for its economic or political misdeeds, and has nurtured an officer corps that has no culture of military subordination to civilian constitutional rule.

The position of the armed forces vis-à-vis human rights violations is best summed up by the written response to a court inquiry by retired Lieutenant General Hugo Chiappe Posse and Brigadier General José Pérez Caldas, who mention "a state of necessity" produced by the "existence in the country of an institutional political situation of a severity unknown until then which justified the utilization of all means of exception on the part of the power of the state." The legal situation imposed by the military was described as one that would "ensure the continuation of state action—the restoration of public power, the consolidation of public peace and defense of the liberty of the fatherland."

This view of events was reiterated when, in the face of several amnesty bills introduced in parliament, almost all the generals who served during the dictatorship signed a letter to President Sanguinetti indicating that they had saved the country from Marxist-Leninist terrorism, had accomplished their task with relatively low cost in terms of life or material (especially when compared to other South American countries), and the current attacks on the honor of the armed forces were but the latest attempt by the Left to destroy the one institution that ultimately defends Uruguay from its external and internal enemies.

The military has argued its immunity from prosecutions for human rights violations on the basis of the fact that it acted to fulfill its mission of defending the nation. The generals cite certain key legislation passed by the civilian government as legitimization of their activities. Most specifically, they point to the April 14, 1972, declaration of a state of internal war, and the July 10, 1972, Law of National Security, which created the category of crimes against the state—*de lesa Nación*—as implicitly giving the military extraconstitutional powers in the struggle against subversion.

The military has shown clearly that its ideological position has not changed under civilian rule. In April 1985, the hard-liners, active and retired, within the armed forces and their civilian supporters formed a movement called Acción Democrática Oriental. Jorge Amondaraín, who was subsecretary of the Ministry of Interior under the dictatorship, made the group's first public declaration, which included a denunciation of the chaos that the country was experiencing. Amondaraín stated that Uruguay was following the same path it had taken in the 1960s and that the situation could become similar to that in Nicaragua. He denounced the amnesty of political prisoners, especially the Tupamaros; deplored the positions currently occupied by leftist intellectuals in the university and school system; and indicated that he felt the labor movement was again dominated by Marxists. According to Amondaraín, the police and the military saved the good people of Uruguay from chaos and dictatorship. Amondaraín went on to state that if his group were in power, all Marxist groups would be illegal, and that it is clear that the traditional parties are not capable of protecting "national identity."

The magazine of the army's Club Militar, *El Soldado*, has called the Contadora Group (Venezuela, Colombia, Panama, and Mexico—countries trying to obtain a diplomatic solution to the situation in Central America) "pro-Communist." It has accused the *New York Times* and the *Los Angeles Times* of supporting Cuba and thus the spread of guerrilla subversion in Latin America. Using a strict East-West, cold war optic, the newspaper has supported President Reagan's geopolitical concerns in the region. More recently, *El Soldado* engaged in a vicious attack on President Alfonsín of Argentina, depicting the human rights trials as the work of a vengeful president who is merely doing the bidding of the international Communist conspiracy found in Moscow and New York. Petitions have begun to circulate at the Club Militar, calling for the army to close ranks and protect those accused of human rights violations. Such activity is very similar to events in August of 1972, when 530 officers met at the club and issued a statement in support of the military's role in the struggle against subversion.

The culture of fear produced by the dictatorship continues to haunt the minds of politicians and workers alike. The various intelligence services of the armed forces have deliberately kept up activities that are designed to intimidate the population. One senator within the ruling Colorado party told me that for three nights a car moved back and forth in front of his house, sometimes with its lights off. He finally went out to get the license number and called the captain of the local police precinct, asking him to trace the owner. After hearing the number of the license plate, the police official immediately indicated that the car belonged to an intelligence service. When the senator inquired as to whether he meant SIN (Servicio de Inteligencia Nacional; National Intelligence Service), the official responded, "No, SIFA—Servicio de Inteligencia de las Fuerzas Armadas [Armed Forces' Intelligence Service]."[6] Until that moment this well-connected senator did not know that an organization with this name existed. In fact, SIFA is the principal intelligence service in Uruguay and is under the control of the Uruguayan Joint Chiefs of Staff, the Estado Mayor Conjunto (ESMACO). By June 1986, the Sanguinetti government was quietly trying to see if the military would be willing to have SIFA put under the direct control of the Defense Ministry, which is headed by a civilian.

On the tenth anniversary of the massacre of eight party activists at a local Communist party headquarters in Montevideo in 1976, a sophisticated and powerful bomb exploded outside a party office. Most observers attributed the bombing to a right-wing military or police group. A radio station was called by an individual who took responsibility for the action, announcing that it was intended to let Sanguinetti know that the president was not going to rule with the aid of a "Jewish-Communist cabal."

In a speech delivered before President Sanginetti on Armed Forces Day (May 18,1986), the army chief of staff, General Hugo Medina, asked if the Law of National Pacification, which had been promulgated a year earlier, was totally fair, as the amnesty it gave to the Tupamaros and common criminals did not extend to the military. The general's statement seemed to represent an important change in the military's position on human rights because heretofore they had regarded the subject as nonnegotiable, arguing that they had never violated human rights as they had been engaged in a legal and constitutionally mandated struggle against subversion. General Medina went on to indicate that the military was happy to be reinserted into the institutional life of the country and that although it understands its duties and obligations, it is also conscious of its rights. On the basis of these and other signals, the Colorado government decided to present its amnesty bill for the military and police to parliament.

However, on June 26, a UPI dispatch written from Montevideo caused political shock waves. A reporter present at a dinner involving a dozen active and retired military officers reported extensively on their conversations. According to the article, those present felt, among other things, that they could wait for the civilian government to exhaust its political capital and that some politicians are making it easy for "Marxism to direct various activities in Uruguay." One colonel at the dinner characterized the military's exit from power as a capitulation, and a retired general expressed the opinion that if the military had left office in 1980 after the plebiscite and when the economy was in fairly good shape, it would probably be asked to take over again now, if it had not already done so earlier.

In July an internal army document was leaked to the Brazilian and Uruguayan press that showed the military's continued preoccupation with national security and its fixation on the possibility of renewed subversion. The text began with a series of questions concerning the activities and motives of various organizations or groups, including unions, political parties, the Catholic church, and educational and press institutions. The document showed particular concern with attempts to disparage and/or infiltrate the armed forces. After laying out the parameters of the information required, the intelligence-gathering task was divided among various military units or departments. Of course, the document paid particular attention to the Frente Amplio and, most especially, to the Communist party and small splinter leftist factions such as IDI (Izquierda Democrática Independiente), the PDP (Partido por la Victoria del Pueblo), and the Tupamaros.

The Tupamaros emerged from prison with a conciliatory political line. They declared that the newly established democracy was qualitatively different from the conditions of the late 1960s and early 1970s and that therefore public and open political action and not armed struggle was their proper role. In recognizing the current democratic rules of the game, they did not eliminate armed struggle if future conditions made such a path necessary. The movement's relationship to its political arm in the 1971 elections, the 26 de Marzo movement, led many to believe that the MLN-Tupamaros would, by fusing itself with this group, seek formal entry into the Frente Amplio. When the small but respected Christian Democratic party, as well as others within the Frente Amplio, strenuously opposed the entrance of the Tupamaros, Raúl Sendic, the founder of the guerrilla movement, called for the creation of a "Frente Grande," implying that the Frente Amplio was not seeking the widest possible coalition of progressive forces. He, however, was in no shape to lead the movement; he went to Cuba for corrective surgery on his tongue and mouth, which had been severely mutilated by wounds he received when he was captured in 1972.

The MLN was experiencing difficulty in adjusting to its new reality. As one ex-Tupamaro put it,

> The movement is paying the price of defeat, with the consequent isolation from reality implied by 12 years in prison. And the other price that is being paid has also been suffered by all revolutionary movements of the left in the world: the crisis of the traditional models of the left. No one now buys the Soviet model in the way that they sell it, there are very few that dream of building a new society with a model like that. Neither, whether because of maturity or because of the time that has gone by, can the reality of the Cuban revolution be taken as transplantable. We lack the beacons we used to have whether because of our age or the stage that our country or humanity in general lived through.[7]

In a press interview given to an Argentine journalist, Julio Marenales, one of the founders of the movement, admitted that the Tupamaros had relied too heavily on only one form of action—armed struggle—and that they had not made the necessary effort to develop contacts and work within the mass organizations of the society. He further indicated that additional self-criticism would take place at the Tupamaros' Fourth National Convention, scheduled for September 1986. At their Third National Convention, in September 1985, the Tupamaros defined their goals as land reform, nationalization of the banking and export sectors, and a moratorium on the foreign debt. The convention reiterated the movement's desire to operate legally and in accordance with the rules of a constitutional and democratic political system. The leadership did remind all who would listen that "the dominant classes have shown throughout history that they are willing to erase legality and democracy every time the people threaten their interests and privilege."

Vice president Tarigo responded angrily to a statement by Julio Marenales in which he indicated that guerrilla war would be valid in the face of another advance of fascism in Uruguay. Tarigo angrily reminded all who would listen that the appearance of the guerrillas in Uruguay in 1963 was a "struggle against democracy and not against fascism" and that the people of Uruguay "without the help of the Tupamaros . . . knew how to find a democratic solution that permitted the Tupamaros to leave jail and return from exile."[8]

In a meeting dubbed an "extraordinary convention" held in late July 1986, the MLN-Tupamaros postponed their Fourth National Convention, scheduled for October, until 1987. At the same time a communiqué was issued by José Mujica, the group's secretary-general, which denounced the lack of resolution of the human rights question. The statement went on to warn that if the government and the people are held hostage, threatened, or blackmailed by the military over human rights violations committed during the dictatorship, then the ex-guerrillas might have to rethink their current stance in support of the democratic game. This not-so-veiled threat was immediately denounced by the mainstream press, which argued that the Tupamaros were as misguided as ever because the government was democratic and free to act on all questions. However, if the Tupamaros were overreacting, so were their critics on this issue. It was clear to an objective observer that the threat of military intervention continued to hang over the government as it tried to find a formula for the military's human rights violations that was acceptable to the guilty as well as to those demanding justice—a difficult formula, indeed.

8

Uruguay and the World

As we saw in Chapter 2, Uruguay's foreign relations during its first decades as a sovereign nation were caught up in the continued ambitions of Argentina and Brazil and the frequent appeal by various political factions in Uruguay for the assistance of one of Uruguay's neighbors.

Internal strife in Uruguay contributed to its involvement in the War of the Triple Alliance (1864–1870), in which Paraguay was invaded by the combined armies of Argentina, Brazil, and Uruguay after the Paraguayan dictator Francisco Solano López sent his troops into Argentine territory in order to aid the Blancos in Uruguay against the Colorado government of Venancio Flores. The country's military participation was quite limited, and the war eventually turned into an essentially Brazilian-Paraguayan conflict.

Uruguay declared its neutrality at the outbreak of World War I but quickly protested Germany's declaration of unrestricted submarine warfare. When a common American Republics' position failed to materialize, Uruguay unilaterally broke relations with Germany in October 1917 and revoked its neutral position with regard to the Allies.

As a small nation sandwiched between the two South American giants, Argentina and Brazil, Uruguay has long been a proponent of the sovereign equality of states and an active participant in international and regional organizations. José Batlle's government at the turn of the century led Uruguay on a dignified path of international cooperation. Batlle was a strong proponent of international law and the peaceful settlement of disputes between nations as the best defense of the sovereignty of small states. At the Hague Peace Conference in 1907, Batlle proposed the creation of an organization that was remarkably similar to the subsequent League of Nations. In 1921, Uruguayan law formally recognized the jurisdiction of the International Court of Justice at the Hague.

113

Uruguay has historically been a forceful advocate of regional international cooperation on economic and social matters. In 1920, President Baltasar Brum proposed the creation of an American League of Nations, which would cooperate with the Geneva-based League—of which Uruguay was a charter member—but would have the authority and responsibility for dealing with problems in the Americas. Uruguay frequently played the role of mediator in the inter-American system, for example as the coordinator of the Pan American Commission of Neutrals, which attempted to mediate the Chaco War between Bolivia and Paraguay in the 1930s. Uruguay joined the Rio Treaty in 1947, and Uruguayan diplomat José A. Mora served as secretary-general of the Organization of American States during 1958–1968. Uruguay was a founding member of the now-defunct Latin American Free Trade Association (LAFTA), which was headquartered in Montevideo. The Charter of Punta del Este, which set up the Alliance for Progress, was signed in Montevideo in 1961.

In 1936 Uruguay became the first nation in Latin America to establish relations with the Soviet Union. In December 1939 the German battleship *Graf Spee* was trapped by British warships in the Río de la Plata and sought refuge in Montevideo harbor. The Uruguayan government refused the ship an extended stay, and it was scuttled by its crew outside the harbor rather than be surrendered to or sunk by the British. The Blanco leader, Luis Alberto de Herrera, protested Uruguay's increasingly anti-Axis position, arguing that the German threat to Latin America was negligible whereas North America's hegemonic design on the continent must be taken seriously.

Uruguay supported the creation of the United Nations and has acted with dignity and social conscience as a member. For instance, on the issue of full employment, the Uruguayan delegation at the fifth General Assembly of the UN argued that "nowadays it is impossible to conceive of individual liberty unless it has the economic support of a guaranteed permanent and remunerative job for every able-bodied man in conditions appropriate to the proper fulfillment of the human personality."[1]

RELATIONS WITH BRAZIL AND ARGENTINA

An integral part of the Uruguayan government's international trade policy has been an attempt to increase bilateral trade relations with the countries of the Southern Cone.[2]

Uruguay has always been concerned with its bilateral relations with Argentina and Brazil. These relations were strained in the 1950s with Argentina when opponents of Peronism sought refuge in Uruguay and promoted a return to democracy in Argentina from the vantage of a democratic and civilian Uruguay. In the 1960s similar strains developed with the Brazilian military regime, especially when Leonel Brizola came to Uruguay to live in exile. Nevertheless, the need for economic integration and the development of hydroelectric resources along the common waterways with Brazil and Argentina led to closer cooperation between Uruguay and its neighbors under the successive governments of Pacheco Areco, Bordaberry, and the military regime. This trend has been accelerated under the new civilian government. The Paysandú-Colón Bridge with Argentina and the joint Brazilian-Uruguayan development of the Guaira Falls hydroelectric project are examples of this cooperation.

Cooperation is institutionalized with both Argentina and Brazil, in the Uruguayan-Argentine Economic Cooperation Agreement dated August 24, 1974, and in the Trade Expansion Protocol dated June 12, 1975, under the Trade Cooperation and Friendship Treaty entered into with Brazil. The objectives of the bilateral agreements are (1) to expand and diversify commercial trade, (2) to stimulate and coordinate investments, and (3) to foster regional integration through joint infrastructure projects.[3] The most effective instruments for achieving these objectives have been the mutual granting of tariff concessions on selected products and the creation of credit lines to finance Uruguayan imports of capital goods from these two countries. Through the initial agreements and subsequent negotiations, Uruguay has obtained duty-free concessions from Argentina for 895 products and about 600 concessions from Brazil with tariff levels ranging below 4 percent. Among the most important Uruguayan exports benefiting from preferential access to the Argentine and Brazilian markets are paper products, chemicals, plastics, textiles, tires, ceramics, processed foods, and appliances.

Although significant regional integration had been achieved (32 percent of total Uruguayan exports in 1980 went to Brazil and Argentina), negotiations were initiated in 1980 for the possible establishment of a comprehensive free-trade union with Argentina. The Uruguayan government position was clearly given in a May 1980 speech by Minister of Economy Valentín Arismendi. He commented that self-sustained economic growth based on exports was impossible under the present international economic situation for two basic reasons. First, the small domestic market of Uruguay simply did not provide the minimum internal market necessary for sustained export growth; and second, Uruguay was facing increased protective cooperation between foreign countries on trade matters (for example, the European Economic Community), a trend that will make it more difficult for Uruguay to develop export markets. In view of these developments, Arismendi claimed that Uruguay's only hope for self-sustained growth based on exports was to broaden the market for its products through an economic union with a larger country, in this case Argentina.[4]

Negotiations during 1980 focused on the legal and functional framework to be established rather than on a detailed discussion of commodity lists. Major points of contention at the technical level were definition of origin, export incentives, and some kind of escape or safeguard clause. The country of origin question became important because the values of foreign origin components in Uruguayan manufactured products tend to be considerably higher than in Argentine ones. The escape clause was requested by the Uruguayan government to win the support of worried businesspeople. In fact, the Uruguayan government seemed much more interested in the integration negotiations than was the local business community. The business community in Uruguay is generally fearful of Argentine competition, believing the much larger Argentine capacity would overwhelm Uruguayan industrial and agricultural producers. Uruguayan entrepreneurs, instead of viewing integration as an opportunity to expand their markets, seem to focus completely on the unexpected flood of products coming from Argentina.

On March 16, 1981, Arismendi and Argentine Minister of Commerce Alejandro Estrada signed a joint declaration in which both countries agreed that the free-trade zone should enter into force as soon as possible. The declaration established a binational technical group, consisting of high officials designated by each government, to recommend specific provisions of a draft agreement setting up such a free-trade zone. However, since that time negotiations have been practically suspended. The economic and political turmoil in Argentina as well as the increasing economic problems in Uruguay were not conducive to further integration. It remained for the Sanguinetti government to bring renewed vigor to the process.

THE SEARCH FOR DIGNITY AND MARKETS

Foreign policy under President Sanguinetti has been guided and inspired by Enrique Iglesias. The policy has been a judicious blend of bilateral, regional, and multilateral activities. Building on a national policy of strengthening democracy, tolerance, and understanding, the government has sought a consensus on foreign policy goals while attempting to strengthen and improve the career foreign service.

Although the military government did attempt to improve trade relations and promote integration with Brazil and Argentina, its overall diplomatic efforts were colored by its reactionary ideology. Uruguay was one of only a handful of countries to send a delegation to South Africa for the apartheid government's granting of "Homeland" status to the

Enrique V. Iglesias, minister for foreign affairs of Uruguay, addressing the forty-first regular session of the United Nations General Assembly in early October 1986 (UN photo 168724/Saw Lwin).

Transkei. As relations deteriorated with the United States over Uruguay's dismal human rights record during the Carter presidency, Montevideo threatened to pull out of the Rio Treaty and support the creation of a South Atlantic Treaty Organization that would include South Africa. The military government refused for years to allow visits by the Red Cross and denounced the European Parliament and such organizations as the International Red Cross and Amnesty International for their denunciations of the human rights record of the regime.

The Ministry of Foreign Affairs has not been noted for a high degree of professionalism. Until recently there was no formal entrance exam for the foreign service and no formal standards concerning previous education or expertise. Under Iglesias this situation has changed somewhat. A formal postgraduate track has been instituted at the Instituto de Profesores Artigas, and there has been an upgrading of the international economic and commercial section of the chancellery. A new office building has been put into use behind the elegant but technologically outdated Palacio Santos, which houses the Ministry of Foreign Affairs.

Iglesias believes that a foreign policy must be principled, pragmatic, and realistic. Uruguay is not going to have international weight because of its size or economic power but because of what it stands for and what it historically represents: the defense of international law, an option for negotiations over the use of force, and support for human rights. Not surprisingly, given his background, the Foreign Ministry under Iglesias has also developed a strong profile on economic matters. It is deeply involved in promoting new markets for Uruguayan exports and attracting foreign investments. Iglesias visited South Korea during his first months in office and sent a high-level trade mission to the People's Republic of China. At the same time, bilateral relations with Uruguay's two neighbors, Brazil and Argentina, were pushed aggressively. The close relationship between presidents Alfonsín and Sanguinetti and their respective foreign ministers resulted in an extraordinary agreement that gives Uruguay duty-free entrance to the Argentine market for up to 5 percent of total Argentine production on a wide range of products. This agreement, known as the Convenio Argentina-Uruguay de Cooperación Económica (CAUCE), entered into force in September 1985.

Sanguinetti was the first president in Uruguay's history to attend the opening of the UN General Assembly. He was also involved with important conversations with U.S. Treasury Secretary James Baker that took place in Peru during the inauguration of Alan García. It was after these meetings that Baker announced a switch in policy on Third World debt, reflecting U.S. acceptance of the Latin American debtors' argument that only growth and not continued austerity will allow them to service their enormous debt while permitting a stable democratic environment.

Iglesias and Sanguinetti feel that a country of 3 million people can have only one dynamic path to growth—exports. This does not mean to say that industry should not produce for the domestic market or that internal distribution of products is not important, but the government believes that the economic well-being of Uruguayan society depends fundamentally on exports.

Exports began to recover in the last quarter of 1985 and in early 1986. This was especially true for the extremely depressed traditional exports of wool and beef. Beef exports were up some 47 percent; fish and seafood, over 80 percent; and leather products increased by some 50 percent in comparison with the same period a year earlier. However, textiles fell slightly during this same time frame. Imports continued at a very reduced level throughout 1985, reflecting the static domestic economic situation. On a year-to-year basis ending in November 1985, imports totaled only $675 million, one of the lowest figures in recent years. In the July 1985 to August 1986 period, exports rebounded to some $960 million.

Uruguay's exports, as important as they are, do not have the weight in the economy that the exports of various other small states have. Exports were 18 percent of GDP in Uruguay in the 1980–1983 period.

TABLE 8.1
1984 Exports

Geographic Destination	Percent
Latin America	26
United States and Canada	15
EEC	20
Middle East	13
Eastern Europe	8
Rest of world	19

Structure of Exports	Percent
Meat	15
Wool	18
Rice	6
Textiles	13
Fruits, cereals, and vegetables	11
Leather	18
Fish	5
Manufactures	14

Source: Banco Central del Uruguay.

The comparable figure for Costa Rica was 34 percent, for Jamaica 50 percent, and for Honduras 32 percent. Among non–Latin American states with a population of 2–5 million, New Zealand showed 29 percent, Israel 49 percent, Finland 34 percent, and Ireland 56 percent. A profile of Uruguay's exports in 1984 may be seen in Table 8.1.

Uruguay's most important trading partners are Brazil, the United States, and Argentina; an oil exporter such as Iran is usually included in the top five. Brazil has emerged as the dominant factor in Uruguay's trade, in part a result of its booming economy in 1985 and 1986. For 1985, exports to Brazil totaled $143 million followed by exports to the United States at $126 million. Together these two markets took over 40 percent of Uruguay's exports. In terms of imports, Brazil was first at $124 million and Iran second at $103 million, followed by Argentina at $83 million. West Germany has moved into the top five of Uruguay's trading partners and stood in third place for the first five months of 1986. During those five months of 1986 exports showed a 24 percent increase over the same period a year earlier, whereas imports only increased by 2.7 percent. The expansion of exports was caused primarily by an increase in the sales of agricultural products and fish.

For Uruguay, the problem of promoting foreign investment is compounded by the country's inability to absorb the capital that is available on an international basis. For Iglesias, the shortage is not of capital—it is a shortage of Uruguayan capitalists. The lack is not of investment capital, but of projects that would attract that investment. Uruguay has the agricultural and livestock resources that, properly utilized, could produce the investment and modernization that would create the "value-added" exports that can meet the government's target of a 50 percent increase in total exports by 1991. This goal cannot be met, however, without a profound modernization of infrastructure and attitudes. As Iglesias has summed it up, "If we are capable of organizing ourselves the world is going to respond; if we do not organize ourselves, the world will leave us aside."[5]

In 1985, the foreign commerce section of the Foreign Ministry targeted nineteen products that could increase total exports some 50 percent over the next five years. In addition, some fifty firms responsible for 90 percent of Uruguay's exports were identified for closer aid and cooperation with the ministry. The very small impact that Uruguay has in global terms—only 1/11,000 of total world trade—is seen as an advantage by Iglesias, as the protectionism rampant in the world may be circumvented by a country like Uruguay, which need only find ten new markets at $50 million each in order to increase its dollar export volume by 50 percent.

During the third week of June 1986, Sanguinetti became the first Uruguayan president in over thirty years to make an official state visit to the United States. In his speech offered at the luncheon given by Secretary of State George Shultz, President Sanguinetti reiterated Uruguay's support for the Contadora process, the UN peacekeeping force in the Sinai in which Uruguay participates, and the struggle against terrorism. But he reserved the bulk of his comments for a discussion of international economic affairs, most especially debt and protectionism. He stressed the fact that the problem of external debt is only one aspect of a deeper issue that is related to international trade, to the transfer of technology, and to solidarity among states. He spoke of the protectionist measures being taken by the European Common Market and the United States. His words on this issue were sophisticated and penetrating and worth quoting at length.

> It must be understood that it is very difficult to put an economy in order as we have done, to cut a budget deficit as we have done, to reduce inflation as we have done, to manage the social tensions that typically develop when a *de facto* government leaves power and, in addition,

to consolidate political democracy—all at one time in an international climate such as the one we have described.

We say that it is very difficult. It is not impossible, but it becomes very difficult. To make our tasks lighter we do not need special subsidies, nor donations, nor international charitable programs. It would be enough if the damages done by those protectionist policies were indemnified and if they were then put aside once and for all assuring us, through agreements, the opportunity to compete as freely as possible on the markets of the developed countries.

Uruguay has an open financial system and a free foreign exchange market because we are convinced that these are the best solutions. We have confidence in our market and so we do not fear capital flight, but we know that to attract more capital, especially investment capital, we must hold out the possibility to produce first and compete later, overseas, on normal, undistorted, markets. It cannot be that we small states are required to cut back on the timid protective steps that we have taken in order to compensate our industrial and agricultural exporters for the lack of technology, the freight rate disadvantages, and the high financial costs while—at the same time—the powerful states, which enjoy those advantages in their competition with our producers accentuate them artificially with aggressive protectionist measures.[6]

At the White House dinner on June 17, 1986, Sanguinetti made the following plea about international trade: "Either international trade opens up or all of us must resign ourselves to live in a new feudalism. The most powerful, perhaps, will cope better, but they will be condemned to live in an aggressive, unstable world full of violence. The smallest countries like us will be condemned to a mediocre life definitively pointing toward poverty."[7]

Although trade policy was the number one agenda item for the delegation from Montevideo, they did not expect to accomplish much on a concrete basis in regard to this issue. The real aim of the trip was to show off Sanguinetti as the cultured and moderate leader who supports a middle-of-the-road capitalist path to development and thus get Uruguay taken more seriously in the future when it presses for trade concessions or seeks positive results on other bilateral or multilateral issues, especially those concerning economic development.

The Frente Amplio's decision to not allow General Seregni to accept President Sanguinetti's invitation to accompany him on the state visit to Washington was criticized harshly by the Socialist and Christian Democratic parties. What is most interesting about the decision is that it was reached by consensus within the political committee of the Frente Amplio despite the objections of Seregni himself, the Socialist and

Christian Democratic parties, and List 99, which by itself had received 40 percent of the Frente's vote in the 1984 election. The decision is thus a good example of how the far Left inside the Frente frequently can force the coalition into negative and uncooperative stances. Many moderates within the Left have publicly argued that the decision hurt the credibility of a movement that was trying to present itself as a viable alternative power in the country. The Socialists, especially, felt the Frente had lost an opportunity to legitimize its role as a leftist opposition coalition capable of interacting with Washington.

Sanguinetti was well received in Washington and made a good impression. Relations between the U.S. embassy and the government in Montevideo have improved under the current U.S. ambassador, Malcolm Wilkey, a retired Republican judge from Arizona. He replaced an even more conservative Southwestern political appointee, Thomas Aranda, Jr. Neither man had any previous diplomatic experience, but Wilkey had been the Kennicott Corporation's chief counsel in Santiago, Chile, in 1970. Ambassador Wilkey does seem to be more politically adept than Aranda, who managed to antagonize almost all political groups during his tenure in Montevideo.

Under Sanguinetti and Iglesias, Uruguay has been supportive of the Contadora process and an active participant in the Cartagena Consensus, which has attempted to formulate a common Latin American position on the debt question. In addition, diplomatic relations were reestablished with Cuba. Iglesias has carefully guided these forays into sensitive regional political issues, leaving more controversial statements and actions to individual politicians whose actions do not reflect official government policy. For instance, young Colorado deputy, Roberto Asiaín, the 1986 president of the Foreign Affairs Committee of Uruguay's Chamber of Deputies, declared during an International Parliamentary Assembly meeting in Chile, that the Pinochet government was not carrying out the transition to democracy that it had promised. "This is a transition from one kind of dictatorship to another that is even more ferocious," Asiaín observed at a press conference. Several weeks later he accompanied Roberto Laino, exiled Paraguayan political leader, on his attempt to return to Asunción from Montevideo.

ONGOING DEVELOPMENTS

At the end of July 1986, Brazil and Argentina signed eleven trade protocols designed to establish the framework for the economic integration of the two countries. The most important short-term agreement involved a commitment by Brazil to purchase 1.375 million tons of Argentine wheat in 1987 and even more in subsequent years. The two countries also agreed to gradually open their capital-goods markets to each other's products on an increasingly duty-free basis. Presidents Alfonsín and José Sarney called on other Latin American nations to join them in the agreements. Uruguay immediately responded to the invitation. In fact, Sanguinetti was the only head of state invited to join the Argentine and Brazilian presidents during their final negotiations in Buenos Aires. The inclusion of Sanguinetti, who was due to meet with Sarney in Brazil in August, fueled speculation that there would be increased momentum toward the creation of a Southern Cone common market. The importance of Brazilian and Argentine trade to Uruguay is highlighted by the fact that Uruguayan trade with Brazil had increased substantially since 1984 because of the slowdown in the Argentine economy produced by the Plan Austral (the Argentine plan to control inflation and ensure the value of the new currency—the *austral*).

In fact, after an extensive series of preparatory meetings, Sanguinetti flew to Brasilia, where on August 13 in the Palacio de Planalto he signed a far-reaching set of agreements, the most important of which expanded the existing Commercial Expansion Protocol (PEC) between the two nations. Under the terms of the new agreement, Uruguay will receive much higher quotas for the export of various meat, rice and dairy products to Brazil. In return, Brazil will receive preferential treatment for the export of capital goods and equipment (for example, buses exempt from import duties) into the Uruguayan market for those products not produced locally in Uruguay. Foreign Minister Iglesias predicted that Uruguay's exports to Brazil would reach $200 million in 1986 and double within the next two years. In 1986 Brazil replaced the United States as Uruguay's largest trading partner and is one with whom Uruguay has a substantial positive trade balance.

There has been much discussion in recent years about Uruguay becoming a free-market zone for trade, banking, and manufacturing, thus making use of its strategic location between Brazil and Argentina. The free convertibility of currency and the unfettered transfer of funds from the country, both of which have been long-standing features of the Uruguayan economy, make such a scheme feasible and attractive. The use of Montevideo's excellent harbor as a free port and the construction of a bridge across the Río de la Plata between Buenos Aires and Colonia in Uruguay are projects that have received increasing attention in recent years. The possibility that Uruguay would become the fruit and vegetable supplier for greater Buenos Aires is very much dependent on the construction of this bridge and may be tied to the use of the harbor of Montevideo by Argentina. The agreements between Brazil and Argentina and between Uruguay and its two larger neighbors make Brazil a "natural" market for Uruguay's cereals, textiles, and leather, which will tie Uruguay's peso more closely to the Brazilian cruzado.

One must of course be quite cautious about any new trade or common-market-type arrangement in Latin America given the sad history of LAFTA and the Central American Common Market, but the recent agreements hold much promise. Brazil and Argentina are the largest markets in South America, and Uruguay's geographic position and nonthreatening economic clout make it easier to see the possibility of its tagging along with its giant neighbors as they attempt to integrate their economies.

9

Conclusions: Return or Renewal?

Philip Taylor acerbically commented over two decades ago that in Uruguay "politics seem in fact, to be the baroque product of sophisticated people without enough to occupy their time."[1] That Uruguay remained a democracy in the face of the economic and social crises of the late 1950s and 1960s is a tribute to its political culture. That it returned to a constitutional system in the manner I have described in this book is a confirmation of that democratic heritage. However, the acquiescence of public opinion in the military's aggrandizement of power in the early 1970s shows that when economic and physical security are threatened, people can put heritage aside. Uruguay easily lost its designation as one of the world's "great leaders of the democratic way of life."[2]

The major questions we must ask in addressing the future of democracy in Uruguay are: Is the reestablishment of democracy based on looking backward with nostalgia toward the past, or is it based on recognizing the reasons for the democratic breakdown and the changes that have taken place in Uruguay and the world during the twelve years of dictatorship? Are the political and economic elites of the society willing to build an innovative and stable future, or will they assume the status quo orientation so prevalent in the 1950s and 1960s? In sum, has Uruguay undergone a restoration or has it embarked on a bold renovation?

The answers seem clear and do not lead one to be overly optimistic. Almost all that has occurred in Uruguay since the military decided to exit and a civilian government took over in March of 1984 feels and smells like a return to the past.

One symptom of this restoration is that, unlike the experience of redemocratization in Spain, Brazil, or Argentina, no new national or extra-party symbol has been developed as an indication that something different is being built. There is no slogan like "Nunca Más" (never again) as there is in Argentina; there is no Plan Austral or Plano Cruzado; there is merely the traditional rhetoric of the parties and their leaders,

125

The past and future meet. Photo courtesy of National Office for Public Relations of the Oriental Republic of Uruguay.

the same old faces with mostly the same old vocabulary. This is as true for the governing Colorados as it is for the leftist opposition and the Blancos, as well as for the leaders of labor and the university.

It is clear that of all the cases of redemocratization in the Southern Cone, the Uruguayan experience has been the closest to an almost total restoration of the previous system. In Brazil, a long drawn out *abertura* included the creation of new political parties and groups and structural changes of enormous magnitude in the economy. In Argentina, the armed forces virtually collapsed as an institution after the Malvinas war, leaving the door open for the dramatic human rights trials that have taken place under a government run by a rejuvenated Radical party.

In Uruguay, the military took a political system that had given the country an exceptionally stable and constitutional political life and put it in a state of suspended animation. At the same time that the generals froze the system, they failed totally in their efforts to coopt leaders or sectors of the traditional parties. The public rejected the military's two electoral attempts to perpetuate a constitutionalized role for itself in Uruguayan political life. The stop-and-start negotiations that culminated in the Pacto de Club Naval restored the old constitution and the byzantine electoral system that the military had attempted to replace from day one of its intervention. The failure of the military project is made complete by its total failure to reorient the economy or provide any sustained effort at economic modernization or growth. Thus in the Uruguayan case we do not see the economic development of Brazil or the discredited military of Argentina. We do see a return to civilian government, a broken economy, and a military that does not wish to pay for any of its crimes or mistakes.

THE MILITARY: WAITING IN THE WINGS?

Of the three military regimes in Argentina, Brazil, and Uruguay, only the Brazilian generals really carried out the twin goals of the national security doctrine—security and development. Brazil's foreign loans and domestic savings found their way into the economy, unlike the situation in Argentina, where the borrowed funds left as massive flight capital almost as fast as they came in. Brazil's military planned their exit well, with a reciprocal amnesty in 1979 ensuring their unscathed departure from power. The Argentine military's disastrous Malvinas adventure and economic malfeasance served to expose them to trials for human rights and other abuses. As usual, the Uruguayan case falls somewhere in between. After their defeat in the 1980 plebiscite, the generals knew they would ultimately give up power (or at least share it). Nevertheless they managed to hold on to power for another four years and would prevent the candidacies of General Seregni of the Frente Amplio and their most outspoken critic, Wilson Ferreira Aldunate of the Blancos. They undoubtedly made it clear to the incoming Colorado government of Julio María Sanguinetti that they would not tolerate being judged for their actions while in power.

The military brass are keen to defend their professional status and to continue to control the military educational system and thereby the socialization process through which officers are recruited and trained. They also wish to continue to receive the disproportionate share of the budget to which they have become accustomed since the early 1970s. In 1983 the budgets of the Defense and Interior Ministries represented some 7.7 percent of GDP and 30 percent of all government expenditures.

The military is not prepared to intervene in economic and social policy with the possible exception of a sudden swing to the Left in such policies, an event that is highly unlikely under the current government. The armed forces may be willing to intervene if they feel their compatriots are about to be judged for human rights violations in an open-ended process that could call into question the legitimacy of the military as an institution.

The generals returned to the barracks in 1984 with a clear sense that they lacked popular support and that their political and economic project was a disaster. But they did not feel that their national security ideology had been discredited nor that they had experienced any defeat in a narrow military sense. This has helped make the human rights violations of the dictatorship an increasingly hot political issue. It is clear that the negotiated military exit had implicit in it an understanding that there would be no move by the incoming government to try any officers or seek to judge the actions of the military as an institution. The Sanguinetti government ignored the issue during its first year in office, hoping that the few civilian cases brought would never go to trial. But the public's interest in the theme, especially as it concerns the murder of popular exiled politicians Zelmar Michelini and Héctor Gutiérrez Ruiz, has been easily manipulated by the leftist opposition, as well as by some figures more connected with the establishment, into a demand for justice that will simply not go away.

As long as the military continues to use national security doctrine, with its struggle against "insurgency" or "subversion," as a justification for human rights violations, the armed forces will continue to be not only one more political party but, in fact, the arbiter of the political game, a fact that is extremely ominous for the future of democracy in Uruguay.

Latin American politics has shown conclusively that the military should not be viewed binominally as either part of government or as a neutral outsider. They may have been the latter for over fifty years of twentieth century Uruguayan politics, but the record of the last twenty years shows a growing political role culminating in a complete takeover and resulting in twelve years of military dictatorship. The restoration of a constitutional system has not meant that the military's influence is again that of a neutral outsider. The Pandora's box of military intervention has been opened in Uruguay. Minimally, the military may be seen as exercising a veto power over government action in such areas as military budgets and personnel, as well as in the far more sensitive and emotional issue of human rights. Maximally, the military may one day decide to again become the direct arbiter of state action according to its own peculiar vision of the nation.

The military's relationship to the political system may be summarized according to the following scale:

Military totally subordinated to civilian rule	Military as veto group	Military as tutelary power	Military government

After many years, if not decades, of military government in most nations of the region, a transition to civilian rule not based on the revolutionary destruction of the armed forces must assume that minimally the military will continue to act as a veto group. It is clear that this has been the case in the region; a recent example is the "resolution" of the human rights legacy in Argentina and Uruguay. The question quickly becomes whether the military will move beyond the exercise of a veto power and choose to take on a tutelary role in such areas as economic policy and labor relations. The probability of such a move increases as the economic situation deteriorates and/or political uncertainties increase.

It is clear that the possibility of direct military intervention will diminish if the economic performance of the civilian regime keeps social tensions at a tolerable level. A review of military intervention in Latin America shows that the armed forces do not usually intervene when the economic situation is stable or improving.

The civilianization of governments does not, however, necessarily mean a return to "democratic normality." To paraphrase Alain Rouquié, the civilianization of the military state is not the same as the demilitarization of power.[3] (Or, put another way, the demilitarization of government is not the same as the democratization of power.) If barriers are to be established for preventing a return to military rule, they will only be erected over time. Time will be required to resocialize the armed forces. Time will be required to legitimize civilian governmental institutions and processes. A key to the successful civilianization of power must involve the public accountability of the military for human rights abuses perpetrated while they ruled. To do less would invite impunity and a sense of immunity on the part of the military, which would make a future intervention more likely.

POLITICS AND THE ELECTORAL GAME IN URUGUAY

Political competition and maneuvering will also bear heavily on the prospects for the consolidation of democracy. There is a five-year interval between elections under Uruguay's constitution, including elections for parliament and all local offices. Wilson Ferreira Aldunate's presidential ambitions may lead him to a strategy of promoting constitutional and electoral reform that would compel Sanguinetti to call elections prior to November 1989. To be successful, such a move requires the cooperation of the Left, which could be amenable, especially if local elections were separated from national elections. Such an arrangement would strengthen the Frente Amplio at the polls and probably give the Left mayoral control of Montevideo. These electoral changes would require a two-thirds vote in parliament. The Colorados have the votes to block such changes, but Wilson and the Left could quickly raise the issue of the very legitimacy of Sanguinetti's election in view of the prohibition on certain candidates imposed by the military in the November 1984 elections.

A reform of the electoral system is long overdue. Uruguayans point with pride to the democracy inherent in their system of the double simultaneous ballot, but we have seen the drawbacks produced by this arrangement.

The 1971 election was a questionable exercise in democracy. The 1984 election took place with the leaders of two of the three parties prohibited from running, although their factions could participate. The parties are already beginning to maneuver with an eye toward 1989 and possible changes in the electoral law. The key players are emerging, and some trial balloons are in the air. The party conventions in 1988 will be based on the 1984 election results. The parties are continuing their same old games of electoral maneuvering. Less than three years into a civilian government and with no elections scheduled until November 1989, the major players are already positioning and posturing in order to maximize their future chances. The feeling seems to be that it was enough to reestablish democracy. Politics as usual justifies itself after the dictatorial experience of the past, even if this means a return to the status quo ante that at its worst was a political and economic stalemate that helped destroy democracy.

The Blancos continue to be led by Wilson Ferreira Aldunate, whose desire to be president cannot be overestimated. His son, Juan Raúl Ferreira, has rapidly increased his status and if Wilson passed from the scene would undoubtedly contest the future leadership of the party with Senator Luís Lacalle, head of an important conservative faction of the Blancos.

In June 1985, Wilson Ferreira Aldunate published a book, *El Exilio y la Lucha*, which analyzed the reasons for Uruguay's decline into dictatorship and his own experiences and actions while in exile. Wilson feels that by the time the 1973 coup took place, liberty was no longer in vogue in Uruguay. "It was threatened, not only by its enemies but also by those who had become exhausted. Not only by those who did not believe in it, but also by those who, invoking it, believed themselves to be more intelligent than the average person and that they could come to power by a shortcut and not by the natural path of obtaining majorities." Wilson is a committed democrat who may be Uruguay's last great caudillo.

Unfortunately, Wilson Ferreira Aldunate's poor health raises serious doubts concerning his ability to unite the Blancos and head their presidential ticket in 1989. A split in the Blancos between a center-left faction headed by Senator Carlos Julio Pereyra and a conservative wing led by Senator Luis Lacalle—with Wilson's son, Senator Juan Raúl

Ferreira trying to inherit his father's mantle—will certainly benefit the Colorado party in the 1989 elections. At the same time, however, such a split in the opposition party will complicate President Sanguinetti's ability to get his programs through a parliament in which the Blancos frequently hold the crucial swing votes.

Senator Hugo Batalla is the popular head of List 99—El Partido Por el Gobierno del Pueblo (Party for a People's Government)—the most-voted faction of the Frente Amplio in the 1984 elections. He is a worthy heir to the group's founder, Zelmar Michelini, and an articulate social democrat. For Batalla, socialism must be built with liberty and with the consent of the majority. The Socialist party under Senator José Pedro Cardoso has slowly moved away from a dogmatic Marxist-Leninist position. It has been willing to criticize the Soviet Union on such issues as Afghanistan. There has been some political speculation that the Socialists may merge with List 99 before the 1989 elections.

List 99 became a full-fledged party at its convention in August 1986. It aspires to be a broad-based, publicly acceptable Socialist party. In terms of future elections, the party's most important project is an electoral reform proposal that would separate parliamentary elections from those for the presidency and would not permit the accumulation of votes by party factions in the presidential elections. Their project would provide a mechanism for a runoff election (ballotage) if no presidential candidate received a requisite percentage of the total vote. Wilson Ferreira Aldunate has also proposed the adoption of the system of ballotage. During the November 1984 elections, Juan Raúl Ferreira called for electoral reforms that would include only one candidate for the presidency from each party and the separation of local from national elections.[4]

The Left, ostensibly united in the Frente Amplio, is divided into three main tendencies. The social democratic wing is dominated, at least in terms of electoral strength, by List 99, headed by Hugo Batalla, but also consists of the Socialist party, led by José Pedro Cardoso, and the Christian Democratic party, which did extremely poorly in the 1984 elections. To the left of this group is the Communist party, still run by Rodney Arismendi and his apparent heir, Jaime Pérez. On the far Left is a wide array of very small groups, the most well known of which is IDI, the Izquierda Democrática Independiente, headed by Alba Roballo.

The social democratic wing wants the Frente Amplio to become a viable alternative to Colorado or Blanco rule. They want the Frente to replace the Blancos as the second most important party in the country and eventually challenge the Colorados for control of government. The Communist party continues to practice an opposition, antisystem politics and would probably like the Frente to follow in this mold. The far Left continues to be as unrealistic as it is unimportant in the scheme of party politics. During 1986, the Frente Amplio restructured itself, creating a Plenario and Mesa de Consulta in an attempt to achieve a working consensus when various political issues arose that frequently split the coalition. The Frente, however, consists of such disparate elements that it is difficult to conceive of a smooth internal governance.

Clouding the picture for the Left then is the salient fact that it consists of a wide range of parties and movements that are ideologically disparate and politically unsure of whether to act as a future alternative government or as a perpetual antisystem gadfly. In addition to the social democratic List 99 and the Communist and Socialist parties, as of late 1986 the Frente Amplio consisted of nine other separate factions, with eight additional groups petitioning for entrance. These latter elements included: The MLN-Tupamaros; Movimiento de Independientes 26 de Marzo, a group that is affiliated with the Tupamaros; Movimiento Revolucionario Oriental (MRO); Movimiento de Independientes Grito de Asencio (MIGDA); Partido Socialista de los Trabajadores (PST); Movimiento de Integración (MI); Partido Obrero Revolucionario (POR); and the Corriente de Unidad Frenteamplista (CUF). All of these groups, like the other smaller factions already in the Frente, are minuscule in size and in electoral strength. However, the Tupamaros and their 26 de Marzo support group continue to be an extremely controversial organization commanding a lot of attention in the press and public opinion, almost all of it negative. The Christian Democratic party, a member of the Frente Amplio, has consistently indicated that it would vote against the entrance into the coalition of any Tupamaro faction.

As for the Colorados, Vice President Enrique Tarigo would seem to be in the best position to be the Colorado candidate in the 1989 election. He is secretary-general of the party and codirector of the most important Colorado newspaper, *El Día*. However, he is not charismatic and would not make a particularly attractive candidate. Politically, he can be accurately described as a liberal and, although he defines himself as a social democrat on economic issues, his position is one of cautious fiscal conservatism based on a desire to streamline the state bureaucracy. Tarigo lacks Sanguinetti's charisma, and for that reason many believe that a younger figure, such as Minister of Labor Hugo Fernández Faingold or Senator Manuel Flores Silva, could emerge with the nomination, or at least the vice presidential slot. Senator Jorge Batlle, a senior statesman in the party, has presidential ambitions but does not enjoy widespread support among the rank and file.

Political families are not new to Uruguay. The almost-twelve-year dictatorship did not dampen this tendency. Jorge Batlle, grandnephew of José Batlle and son of Luis Batlle Berres, is a Colorado senator and continues to be a major force in the party. Manuel Flores Silva, son of deceased Colorado Senator Flores Mora, is a young and upcoming senator in the ruling party. Luis Lacalle, a Blanco senator, is the grandson of the great Blanco caudillo and political leader Luis Alberto de Herrera. Juan Raúl Ferreira is the son of Wilson Ferreira. Rafael Michelini, one of the sons of the assassinated Zelmar Michelini, has begun a political career and has been elected to the local government in the Department of Montevideo.

POLITICAL CULTURE, ECONOMICS, AND THE FUTURE

The military failed, on all levels, to carry out its mission. It could not destroy the Left, create a self-sustaining economy, nor eliminate the bourgeois political system it detested as having been midwife to the birth of the Left. The torture, murder, and culture of fear the dictatorship created is amply documented, first, outside of Uruguay, and more recently, within.

The political culture of Uruguay stresses democracy and individual freedom, but it is not strong on national unity or in identifying individual or factional interests with the national interest. On inauguration day, as many people flew party flags or flags representing political groups as flew Uruguay's national flag. The failure to have a vision of the nation that includes everyone has haunted Uruguay since the economic decline set in thirty years ago. As I observed in 1975,

> Uruguay's Batllista experiment, as limited as it may have been, was an attempt to build a viable nation-state. The democratic nationalism which it propounded and the policies and institutions which it established gave the Uruguayan citizen a standard of living, a freedom of conscience, and quality of membership in the social nation that would be difficult to equal in many systems. The turning away from that commitment in the 1930s put Uruguay on an ever more precarious course in which the Batllista legacy survived as a structure whose facade slowly crumbled as leadership groups tried to maintain their own position and their control of the state without the necessary commitment to the national community which effective action required.[5]

Whether it was the particularist-clientelist politics of the Blancos and Colorados or the isolated, if idealistic, action of the Tupamaros or the speculative and capital flight activities of the business community, no one really concerned themselves with the national interest. The situation was polarized, the actors myopic, and the public socially conservative. It remained for the military, with their narrow but determined definition of the national interest, to take control of the situation.

The military, so long an apolitical institution, decided to play a role we have grown accustomed to in Latin America—that of undertaker in the death of the social nation.

As Luis Costa Bonino has perceptively summed up the last three decades:

> One can say that the contemporary history of Uruguay has seen the failure of three conceptions of the country, of three fragmentary "nationalisms." The first, the old model of the traditional country with a verbal and rickety nationalism always supported by the crutch of co-participation which was not capable of sustaining a durable democracy for the future. The revolutionary nationalism that the MLN urged was, in spite of its "Patria para todos," a conspiratorial and antidemocratic nationalism, symmetrical to that of the military's ideology, an ideology where "traditional parties=oligarchy=North American imperialism" formed an inseparable and ineluctable whole. From the right, the armed forces proposed a homologous conspiratorial nationalism in which Parties or Movements of the left=Parliament=Subversion=the Soviet Union and international communism.
>
> The prognostications for the future of Uruguayan democracy can be very gloomy if there does not emerge in the next few years a new "idea of the country" that is nurtured in all the political parties and that would permit whoever comes to power the ability to make his "politics of party" into a true national politics.[6]

A window of opportunity has opened for the Uruguayan government because of changing international economic conditions. The drop in U.S. interest rates in late 1985 and early 1986 lowered the burden for servicing the debt. Equally as important, the precipitous decline in the price of oil from over $30 a barrel to around $15 during this same time period meant that Uruguay would save some $90 million on its oil import bill. These positive factors, which, of course, could change dramatically in the future, have given the Sanguinetti government some leeway and additional resources with which to stimulate economic recovery.

The old formula of exporting primary products to pay for the capital goods and technology of the industrially advanced countries is dubious at best. The contracting world market for agricultural and mineral products, caused in part by changing technology and increased protectionism, has made this route to development even more precarious than it has been in the past. As has been argued in the 1980s, capital movements rather than trade are the driving force in the world economy. In addition, the two (trade and capital movements) are not as closely linked as they have been in the past, and their relationship has become less predictable. Uruguay is, of course, not going to change economic trends, but it cannot ignore them. If capital movements are to be the new flywheel of the world economy, then Uruguay's position between Brazil and Argentina may be a resource that can be maximized in the future. In fact, this idea is not new, but it has taken on vigorous momentum under the civilian government.

Of particular interest is the question of effective rates of return in various economic activities and the internal and external policies and power relations that establish or change these rates. For decades, government policy in Uruguay and an increasingly hostile international market environment have resulted in economic stagnation. Inflation in this context may be understood as a method for redistributing existing resources and a symptom of the conflict produced between various social and economic groups competing for a share of those shrinking resources. This struggle for the distribution of a stagnant supply of goods and services has resulted in a nominal increase in salaries and income based on the increase in prices. At the level of government macroeconomic policy, the struggle is most manifest in exchange rate policy and demands for salary increases. The two have frequently fed on each other in a vicious spiral that fueled continuous high inflation lasting for years if not decades.

The explanations for inflation in Latin America vary widely, but two competing models generally dominate the literature. The model associated with the IMF has attributed inflation to an increased money supply that creates a demand for goods and services that cannot be met by the productive apparatus of the economy. This exaggerated growth and demand are created by a combination of fiscal deficit, expansion of bank credit, and increases in salaries. The cure includes an austerity program to reduce the deficit and contain wage increases.

The classic dependence model sees inflation as a process resulting from the changes produced in the relations between a peripheral country and international capitalism and the consequences of these changes for investment opportunity and the creation of profit. The usual discussion in this model of the role of multinational corporations is not easily demonstrable for Uruguay, but the arguments concerning terms of trade, external debt, and the return on investment capital are on the mark. Money in Uruguay, at least for those who possess it, has not found a sufficient return as productive capital. Given the extremely liberal financial regulations (free convertibility of currency, etc.), it was easy to put such money to work in the speculative financial arena or simply export dollars to more secure havens. The economic record of the 1970s and 1980s demonstrates that such speculation increased the financial dependence of Uruguay and was paid for in part by the working class and segments of the middle class in the form of reduced purchasing power and reduced opportunity for employment.

The austerity programs put in place under IMF guidelines since 1982 have enabled debtor nations, including Uruguay, to service their debts. The costs, however, have included continued high unemployment and declining standards of living. What is worse, even under the most optimistic of scenarios, debtors face years of slow growth and continuing negative transfers of capital to creditor countries. Under such circumstances the temptation to declare a debt moratorium or to simply default increases. More and more debtor countries are now trading goods through a barter system that does not require short-term financing. Because it does not look like significant flows of new capital will be forthcoming, many such countries might conclude that they do not have that much to lose by defaulting. After all, a default frees up money that would have gone for debt servicing and can now be used to purchase strategic imports and promote more rapid economic growth. However, given the economic and foreign policy team in place in Montevideo, default will not be an Uruguayan-led strategy.

MUDDLING THROUGH

Alain Touraine, the noted French sociologist, made the following observation while on a visit to Montevideo:

> I do not see a strong entrepreneurial spirit (in Uruguay). But because of the size of the country, its high level of technical capacity, of cultural integration, of education, and perhaps because of the weight of its Foreign Minister in the continent . . . it is a country that can . . . at last resolve its problems. What is going to happen with Uruguay, is that it is going to be saved, without saving itself. It is Brazilian growth that is going to save Uruguay.[7]

Ideology and a small and homogeneous population concentrated in one principal city, when coupled with the easy factionalism permitted by the electoral laws, has helped create an atmosphere of accessibility and proximity on which gossip thrives. There are no secrets in Montevideo, and politicians are seen close up, warts and all. Although this has been conducive to sophisticated political games and sharp political humor, it also has helped create the kind of familiarity that does, indeed, breed contempt. As the economic pie continues to shrink, this physical and emotional proximity exacerbates tensions.

It is in this context that we must consider the meaning of anti-communism in Uruguay. Its impact has been especially felt in two areas:

the labor movement and electoral politics. As the economic situation deteriorated, labor organized to protect its interests. Unions have had a long and proud history in Uruguay dating back to the turn of the century. In 1966, a new and more powerful trade union confederation was organized under the leadership of the Communist party—the National Federation of Workers (CNT). Public and private employees began to make direct demands on government for increases in real wages as purchasing power declined drastically in the face of the record inflation of 135 percent in 1967. The number of strikes and work stoppages skyrocketed. The government's response hardened with the use of troops to break a utility workers' strike in 1968 and the militarization of bank employees in 1969. Strikes and labor militancy made for rapidly deteriorating labor-management relations. Uruguay's industrialists would come to view the destruction of the trade union movement as the dictatorship's most significant accomplishment. This was far more important to them than the dismantling of the Tupamaros, whom the industrialists saw as a nuisance but not the threat that the Communist-led unions represented to their interests.

In the brief period of democratic restoration there is little evidence to suggest that Communist influence in the union movement and participation in the Frente Amplio is a comfortable vision of the future to the average Uruguayan, let alone to the political Right and the military.

Intellectuals in Uruguay, as in most of Latin America, are men and women of the Left in overwhelming proportion. Most of them are supporters of one of many factions that make up the Frente Amplio. Unfortunately, this has meant that the Frente, like its intellectual supporters, has not gotten beyond the vocabulary of opposition and negation, a vocabulary not conducive to consensus-building. This may have been the natural vocabulary in the 1960s and early 1970s; it was the only conscionable vocabulary under the dictatorship. But a vocabulary and politics of opposition will not serve well the Uruguay of the present or future—if democracy is to survive.

Marcha lives as *Brecha* and that is as good as it is important. But it is not enough. Intellectuals must learn how to dialogue with the government and the typical Uruguayan. Practical solutions must be offered, not merely rhetoric. Speaking truth to power is essential, but the harsh truths of Uruguay's economic situation are known to all. A creative political breakthrough is needed, and in this regard, the intellectual must be bold, not merely negative and sectarian. Uruguay is a broken country. This is the legacy of the dictatorship. It is a legacy that serves a Fascist military well for the future.

A natural tension between class and nation exists in all social systems, especially those that are capitalist. The strain between loyalty to nation and loyalty to class has been bridged historically by the "myth" of social mobility, which, although recognizing class differences, held up the state as the impersonal regulator of the marketplace of opportunity for all citizens. But the exhaustion of the import-substitution model in Uruguay by the mid-1960s put an extra burden on the public sector. The traditional parties enmeshed in clientelist politics now increasingly used their control of state institutions to satisfy particularistic demands. The state increasingly became a provider rather than an arbiter. As Aldo Solari perceptively observed, "Rather than as a secular artifact destined to resolve social conflicts at the highest level, that state is conceived in a paternalistic manner, as the one who must keep the vigil in order to, in the last analysis, sustain everyone."[8]

The Uruguayans are a dispirited people. They do not have a positive attitude about the future. Some might call this realism. But the intellectual and artistic community must engender a sense of the possible if Uruguayans are to build their lives and their country. They can work with a political culture that is democratic but that has to overcome the sectarianism of the past and the impoverishment of the present. If nothing else, the military forced a cooling-off of a conflict-ridden society. The cost was, of course, unjustifiable, but redemocratization should at least take advantage of the "calming" produced by the dictatorship. Intellectuals along with everyone else must allow conflict to be resolved at the interinstitutional level and not explode into the uncontrolled war of values of the early 1970s.

The system needs time if democracy is to survive. This is not an argument for conservatism or conformity. Any leftist movement in Uruguay, and most especially a revolutionary one, must come to grips with the socially and politically conservative nature of the society. The average Uruguayan is now forty years of age; is fiercely middle class in values, if no longer in income; is nostalgic for the past; and, for better or worse, lacks the *viveza criolla* (native smarts) that one can find among Argentina's *porteños* (people from Buenos Aires). The Frente Amplio may get 30 percent of the vote in Montevideo, but its dismal showing in the interior has condemned it twice in a row to one-fifth of the total vote. Even if a discredited Colorado government and a Blanco party without Wilson Ferreira were to lose to the Left in 1989, it is difficult to believe that the Frente would come to power with more than 35 percent of the vote. Allende's Chile immediately comes to mind. Given the coalition nature of the Frente, one cannot be sanguine about its ability to govern in such a situation.

The Left's task must include outreach to Uruguay's interior. More important, the Left must change its confrontational image. The place to start is with its rhetoric. If in some ways the Sanguinetti government is a *continuista* regime, the opposition is guilty of being a *continuista* opposition. Here the producers of culture have as much responsibility as the politicians. As Mario Benedetti so incisively observed in 1986,

> For those who have the responsibility to govern as well as for those who have the right to oppose them, a minimum level of boldness is necessary. Without courage (which is not imprudence) one does not advance. I feel that in this most decisive moment, a bit of courage is lacking in both the government and the opposition. It is as if the dictatorship had left us without strength. In any case, we have to recover it. One must dare to say no to actual power, internal as well as external. But one also has to dare to say yes, sometimes from above to those below and other times from below to those above. It is not socially healthy to enslave oneself to models whether of any type.
>
> Even inside of and from the Left we must reconsider our language. It is not as important to shout *unity* as it is to act in unity. . . . This also requires courage, an understanding of the *other*, a vocation for truth, and love of country. More and more, I am less pleased with slogans and more pleased with real results. I feel nostalgic for the latter.[9]

Uruguay is now very much part of Latin America in many ways it wasn't, or thought it wasn't, in the past: underdeveloped, dependent, possessed of a politicized right-wing military, and drowning in debt. Democracy's survival will ultimately depend on political and intellectual skill in providing economic growth and social justice along with recently restored civil liberties. Unfortunately, there has also been a restoration of many of the old habits that led Uruguay into its national tragedy. If the lessons of the past two decades are not learned and do not lead to new ideas and new ways of acting, then Uruguay's politicians and intellectuals may be doing nothing more than rearranging the deck chairs on the Titanic.

HUMAN RIGHTS, AMNESTY, AND DEMOCRACY

After the defeat of both the Colorado and Blanco amnesty projects, the political stalemate got progressively worse, reaching its nadir on November 14, 1986, when, for the first time in history, parliament could not pass the budget authorization for the following year. The Sanguinetti government then threatened to call for early congressional elections (the presidency would not be at stake) unless the budget and human rights stalemate could be overcome. By early December, the budgetary impasse had been resolved amidst rumors that the Colorados and Blancos were close to an agreement on an amnesty bill.

Shortly thereafter, the military's top leadership during the dictatorship issued a declaration in which they admitted that "transgressions" had occurred while they were in power. Vice president Tarigo immediately proclaimed the statement to be a human rights confession by the military. The Sanguinetti government also hinted that Uruguay was still in a less than perfect transition period from dictatorship to full democracy. Such an admission was enough to give Wilson Ferreira Aldunate the excuse (albeit an oblique one) to support an amnesty bill, which he had vigorously opposed only months earlier, by claiming that his party was voting for the bill in order to ensure the stability of Uruguay's fragile democracy.

On December 22, the Uruguayan Chamber of Deputies passed, by a vote of 60–37, an amnesty bill that was promptly signed by President Sanguinetti. The legislation in effect prevents the prosecution of any human rights violations committed by military and police personnel during the dictatorship (1973–1985). In addition, the law terminated the thirty-eight cases already pending in the courts.

The legislation was approved after bitter debate in both houses of parliament, fistfights between legislators, and violent street demonstrations. It took effect just one hour before Colonel José Nino Gavazzo was due to appear in court to testify in a case concerning the 1976 abduction of Uruguayan journalist Eduardo Rodríguez Larreta in Argentina and his removal to a detention center in Montevideo. Colonel Gavazzo and the entire military had made it clear that they would not participate in any trials and would ignore or resist any subpoenas to do so. Such refusal would have created a full-blown constitutional crisis between the executive and the armed forces.

The Uruguayan government's failure to find some accounting for the human rights violations of the dictatorship puts the nation's recently restored democracy on a shaky foundation. The armed forces have been sent a signal that reinforces their sense of being above the law. It permits the military to believe that its messianic vision of national security justifies its continued monitoring of the political situation and gives it a clearer path to intervention in the future. Equally as important, support for democracy has been eroded because of the failure of Uruguay's political leaders to come to terms with the past and thus build the future on a firm moral and ethical basis. Uruguayan society will now be further split politically, and if economic growth and well-being are not generated during the remaining years of the Sanguinetti government, social unrest and political instability will likely follow.

Guillermo O'Donnell and Philippe Schmitter have offered several insightful observations on the human rights *problemática:*

> Here we encounter yet another of the paradoxes that plague and enervate these transitions: where and when it is easier to bury the past,

is where and when it is less important to do so. On the contrary, where these "past accounts" are of greater weight and more recent origin and involve a wider spectrum of persons, it is much more difficult and dangerous to attempt to collect them.

But even under the worst of circumstances—heavy and recent occurrence, and heavy and widespread military complicity, as in contemporary Argentina—we believe that the worse of bad solutions would be to try to ignore the issue. Some horrors are too unspeakable and too fresh to permit actors to ignore them. . . . It is difficult to imagine how a society can return to some degree of functioning which would provide social and ideological support for political democracy without somehow coming to terms with the most painful elements of its own past. By refusing to confront and to purge itself of its worst fears and resentments, such a society would be burying not just its past but the very ethical values it needs to make its future livable. Thus, we would argue that, despite the enormous risks it poses, the "least worst" strategy in such extreme cases is to muster the political and personal courage to impose judgment upon those accused of gross violations of human rights under the previous regime. . . .

How the messianic self-image of the armed forces' role and the manipulation of it by civilians can be transformed, is one of the key questions of the transition and one which persists well into the phase of democratic consolidation. The answer depends not only upon whether and how certain actors are punished for their past transgressions, but also upon the lessons everyone draws from the authoritarian experience.[10]

Many Uruguayans agree with these sentiments. On February 22, 1987, a campaign was launched to gather more than 520,000 signatures—one-fourth of the eligible electorate—to put the amnesty law (Law No. 15,848, unofficially known as the "ley de caducidad de la pretensión punitiva del estado" [law renouncing the punitive intention of the state]) to a popular vote. It was unclear whether the proreferendum forces, which include dissident Colorado and Blanco factions as well as the Left, would gather the requisite signatures. It appeared likely that they would and that the country as a whole would debate and vote on the wisdom and ethics of closing the books without a full accounting of the human rights legacy of the dictatorship. No one could say whether such a vote, if it did take place, would overturn the amnesty law or how the military and the civilian leadership would respond to a reopening of the issue. Democracy, by definition, includes a degree of uncertainty and risk. It is strengthened by a citizenry and leaders who understand and accept these conditions.

The amnesty law as a "solution" to the human rights legacy of the dictatorship is another example of less than courageous muddling through. The response may be viewed as a political necessity in the face of a still hard-line military, but, once again, rather than coming to grips with a problem, Uruguay's leaders have chosen to ignore it or postpone its resolution. I sincerely hope that the Sanguinetti government, which, as I have documented in this study, is decent and competent, will demonstrate more courage as it faces the economic and social problems that must be overcome if Uruguay is to consolidate its recently restored democracy and enter the twenty-first century reclaiming its title, the "Switzerland of South America."

Notes

CHAPTER 1

1. Antonio Grompone, *Las clases medias en el Uruguay* (Montevideo: Ediciones de la Plata, 1962), p. 42.
2. (Montevideo: Tipográfica Atlantida, 2nd ed., 1946).

CHAPTER 2

1. Simon G. Hanson, *Utopia in Uruguay* (New York: Oxford University Press, 1938), p. 3.

CHAPTER 3

1. *El Día*, October 24, 1915.
2. *El Día*, September 3, 1919, cited in Simon G. Hanson, *Utopia in Uruguay* (New York: Oxford University Press, 1938), pp. 24–25.
3. Ricardo Martínez Ces, *El Uruguay Batllista* (Montevideo: Ediciones de la Banda Oriental, 1967), pp. 196–197.
4. *Discursos del Dr. José Irureta Goyena* (Montevideo, 1948), cited in Luis C. Benvenuto, "La Quiebra del Modelo," *Encyclopedia Uruguaya*, No. 42 (Montevideo: Editorial Reunidos and Editorial Arca, 1969), p. 156.
5. H. D. [Gilberto Eduardo Perret], *Ensayo de historia patria*, vol. 2: *La República*, 10th ed. (Montevideo: Barreiro y Ramos, 1955), p. 394.
6. *El Día*, August 12, 1916.
7. For a complete discussion of this concept, see Kalman H. Silvert, "The Strategy of the Study of Nationalism," in Kalman H. Silvert, ed., *Expectant Peoples: Nationalism and Development* (New York: Vintage Books, 1967).
8. Luis C. Caviglia, *Estudios sobre la realidad nacional*, vol. 3 (Montevideo: Urta and Curbelo, 1952), p. 73.
9. Martin Weinstein, *Uruguay: The Politics of Failure* (Westport, Conn.: Greenwood Press, 1975), p. 73.
10. Each faction of a party designates its candidates on one sheet, or voting list, on which the faction is given an identifying number. This sheet is

what a voter will put in the ballot box. Thus, a faction comes to be identified by its list number, which appears on all its campaign material. In the case of an important faction that has long been associated with its particular list, such as List 15 (Quince), senators and members of parliament from this faction come to be known by name, as, for example, Quincistas.

CHAPTER 4

1. Aldo Solari, "Las Estructuras Sociales y su Posible Evolución," *Estudios sobre la sociedad uruguaya,* vol. 1 (Montevideo: Editorial Arca, 1967), p. 67.

2. Ronald H. McDonald, "Electoral Politics and Uruguayan Political Decay," *Inter-American Economic Affairs* 26, no. 2 (Summer 1972), p. 44.

3. *Acción,* November 23, 1962, p. 4.

4. "Carta Abierta a la Policía," printed in *Época,* December 7, 1967.

5. *Marcha,* June 5, 1970, pp. 12–15. The translation used here is by Raymond Rosenthal, ed., *State of Siege* (New York: Ballantine Books, 1973), p. 195. This volume is the screenplay and documentary appendix of the Costa-Gavras movie.

6. Luis Costa Bonino, *Crisis de los partidos tradicionales y movimiento revolucionario en el Uruguay* (Montevideo: Ediciones de la Banda Oriental, 1985), *passim.*

7. Martin Weinstein, *Uruguay: The Politics of Failure* (Westport, Conn.: Greenwood Press, 1975), p. 126.

8. Ibid., p. 119.

9. *New York Times,* August 14, 1969.

10. See Howard Handelman, "Labor-Industrial Conflict and the Collapse of Uruguayan Democracy," *Journal of Inter-American Studies and World Affairs* (November 1981), pp. 371–394.

11. Ronald H. McDonald, "The Rise of Military Politics in Uruguay," *Inter-American Economic Affairs* 28, no. 4 (Spring 1975), pp. 41–42.

12. Costa Bonino, *Crisis de los partidos tradicionales,* p. 33.

CHAPTER 5

1. Juan Rial, *Los militares en tanto "Partido Político Sustituto" frente a la redemocratización* (Montevideo: Centro de Informaciones y Estudios del Uruguay, 1985), p. 16.

2. Junta de Comandantes en Jefe, *Las Fuerzas Armadas al Pueblo Oriental: el proceso político* (Montevideo: Las Fuerzas Armadas, 1978), p. 247. Translation is mine.

3. Ibid. and its companion volume, *Las Fuerzas Armadas in Pueblo Oriental: La subversión* (Montevideo: Las Fuerzas Armadas, 1976).

4. For an excellent discussion of these concepts, see Genero Arriazada, "Ideology and Politics in the South American Military: Argentina and Brazil, Chile and Uruguay," (Washington, D.C.: The Wilson Center Latin American Program, Working Paper No. 55).

5. *New York Times*, December 2, 1984.

6. Christopher S. Wren, "Salvaging Lives After Torture," *New York Times Magazine*, August 17, 1986, p. 19.

7. Juan Corradi, "The Mode of Destruction: Terror in Argentina," *Telos*, no. 54 (Winter 1983), p. 68.

8. Cited in the *1980 Report on Uruguay* of the Inter-American Commission on Human Rights (Washington, D.C.: OAS, 1981), p. 128.

9. This discussion of the military's economic policy is adapted from my chapter, "Uruguay: Military Rule and Economic Failure," in Robert Wesson, ed., *Politics, Policies and Economic Development in Latin America* (Stanford, Calif.: Hoover Institution, Stanford University, 1984), pp. 38–52.

10. Mario Blejer and Donald Mathieson, "The Preannouncement of Exchange Rate Changes as a Stabilization Instrument," *IMF Staff Papers* 28, no. 4 (December 1981), p. 761.

11. Ibid., pp. 763–64.

12. República Oriental del Uruguay, Ministry of Economy and Finance, "Economic Opening in Uruguay," *Uruguay Económico* 2, no. 2 (1981), p. 37.

13. Lauren A. Benton, "Reshaping the Urban Core: The Politics of Housing in Authoritarian Uruguay," *Latin American Research Review* 21, no. 2 (1986), p. 48.

14. This section is adapted from a study coauthored with Louise B. Popkin entitled, "A Report on Intellectual, Artistic and Cultural Freedom in Uruguay," *LASA Forum* 14, no. 4, pp. 26–30.

15. Curriculum for training high school principals (Curso de Directores), entitled *Sociología de educación* (Sociology of education). Taught at the Instituto Magisterial Superior and published by CONAE (Consejo Nacional de Educación) in 1976.

16. From interviews conducted by Dr. Louise Popkin in Montevideo.

CHAPTER 6

1. *Correo de los Viernes*, no. 176, September 7, 1984.

2. Juan Rial, *Concertación y gobernabilidad* (Montevideo: CIESU, 1985), DT/124.

3. Foreign Broadcast Information Service, November 16, 1984, p. K4.

CHAPTER 7

1. *Búsqueda*, January 23, 1986, p. 7.

2. Ibid., March 20, 1986, p. 5.

3. Ibid., June 5, 1986, p. 5.

4. Terri Shaw, "M.D.'s in Uruguay Linked to Torture," *Washington Post*, May 23, 1986, pp. A17, 22.

5. *Búsqueda*, July 17, 1986, p. 7.

6. Ibid., June 19, 1986, p. 40.

7. Leo Harari, as reported in *Aquí*, March 11, 1986.

8. *Búsqueda,* January 23, 1986.

CHAPTER 8

1. "El Uruguay en la Quinta Asamblea de las Naciones Unidas," *Marcha,* January 12, 1951. Cited in George Pendle, *Uruguay,* 2nd. ed. (Oxford University Press, 1957), p. 79.

2. This section benefited greatly from discussions with Mark Siegelman of the Office of International Trade Administration, United States Department of Commerce.

3. The World Bank, *Uruguay: Economic Memorandum* (Washington, D.C., 1979), p. 33.

4. Valentín Arismendi, Speech to the American Association of Montevideo, May 22, 1980.

5. Speech to the Centro Comercial de San José, October 11, 1985, p. 17.

6. Speech by President Sanguinetti delivered at luncheon given by U.S. Secretary of State George Schultz, Washington, D.C., June 17, 1986.

7. Speech by President Sanguinetti at White House dinner, Washington, D.C., June 17, 1986.

CHAPTER 9

1. Philip B. Taylor, Jr., *Government and Politics of Uruguay,* Tulane Studies in Political Science, vol. 7 (New Orleans: Tulane University, 1962), Preface.

2. Russell Fitzgibbon, *Uruguay: Portrait of a Democracy* (London: Allen and Unwin, 1956), p. 274.

3. *La Democracia,* no. 79 (November 1, 1984), p. 7.

4. Alain Rouquié, "Demilitarization and the Institutionalization of Military-dominated Politics in Latin America," in Guillermo O'Donnell, Philippe C. Schmitter, and Laurence Whitehead, eds., *Transitions from Authoritarian Rule: Comparative Perspectives* (Baltimore: Johns Hopkins University Press, 1986).

5. Martin Weinstein, *Uruguay: The Politics of Failure* (Westport, Conn.: Greenwood Press, 1975), p. 35.

6. Luis Costa Bonino, *Crisis de los partidos tradicionales y movimiento revolucionario en el Uruguay* (Montevideo: Ediciones de la Banda Oriental, 1985), p. 83.

7. *Búsqueda,* July 25, 1986.

8. Aldo Solari, "Las Estructuras Sociales y su Posible Evolución," *Estudios sobre la sociedad uruguaya,* vol. 1 (Montevideo: Editorial Arca, 1967), p. 167.

9. *Brecha,* January 7, 1986, p. 30.

10. Guillermo O'Donnell and Philippe C. Schmitter, *Transitions from Authoritarian Rule: Tentative Conclusions About Uncertain Democracies* (Baltimore: Johns Hopkins University Press, 1986), pp. 30–31. This is the last of the four paperback volumes in the Transitions series.

Selected Bibliography

César A. Aguiar. *Uruguay: país de emigración.* Montevideo: Ediciones de la Banda Oriental, 1982.

Robert E. Biles. "Patronage Politics: Electoral Behavior in Uruguay." Doctoral thesis, Johns Hopkins University, 1972.

Luis Costa Bonino. *Crisis de los partidos tradicionales y el movimiento revolucionario en el Uruguay.* Montevideo: Ediciones de la Banda Oriental, 1985.

Paul W. Drake and Eduardo Silva, eds. *Elections and Democratization in Latin America, 1980–1985.* San Diego: Center for Iberian and Latin American Studies, University of California, 1986.

M.H.J. Finch. *A Political Economy of Uruguay Since 1870.* New York: St. Martin's Press, 1981.

Rolando Franco. *Democracia "a la uruguaya": analises electoral 1925–1985.* Montevideo: Editorial El Libro Libre, 1984.

María Esther Gilio. *The Tupamaro Guerrillas: The Structure and Strategy of the Urban Guerrilla Movement.* New York: Saturday Review Press, 1972.

Charles Gillespie et al., eds., *Uruguay y la democracia.* 3 vols. Montevideo: The Wilson Center Latin American Program/Ediciones de la Banda Oriental, 1985.

Edy Kaufman. *Uruguay in Transition.* New Brunswick, N.J.: Transaction Books, 1979.

Luis Macadar. *Uruguay 1974–1980: Un nuevo ensayo de reajuste económico?* Montevideo: CINVE/Ediciones de la Banda Oriental, 1982.

Horacio Martorelli. *Transición a la democracia.* Montevideo: Ediciones de la Banda Oriental, 1984.

Banjamin Nahum. *La época batllista (1905–1929).* Montevideo: Ediciones de la Banda Oriental, 1986.

Jorge Notaro. *La Política Económica en el Uruguay (1968–1984).* Montevideo: CIEDUR/Ediciones de la Banda Oriental, 1984.

Guillermo O'Donnell, Philippe C. Schmitter, and Laurence Whitehead, eds. *Transitions from Authoritarian Rule: Latin America.* Baltimore: Johns Hopkins University Press, 1986.

Carina Perelli and Juan Rial. *De mitos y memorias políticas.* Montevideo: Ediciones de la Banda Oriental, 1986.

Porzecanski, Arturo C. *Uruguay's Tupamaros: The Urban Guerrillas.* New York: Frederick A. Praeger, 1973.

Juan Rial. *Partidos políticos, democracia y autoritarismo.* 2 vols. CIESU/Ediciones de la Banda Oriental, 1984.

————. *Uruguay: elecciónes de 1984; Un triunfo del centro.* Montevideo: Ediciones de la Banda Oriental, 1985.

Uruguay. Junta de Comandantes en Jefe. *Las Fuerzas Armadas al Pueblo Oriental: La subversión.* Montevideo: Fuerzas Armadas Uruguayas, 1976.

————. Las Fuerzas Armadas al Pueblo Oriental: El proceso político. Montevideo: Fuerzas Armadas Uruguayas, 1978.

Milton I. Vanger. *The Model Country: José Batlle y Ordóñez of Uruguay (1907–1915).* Hanover, N.H.: Brandeis University Press, 1980.

Martin Weinstein. *Uruguay: The Politics of Failure.* Westport, Conn.: Greenwood Press, 1975.

Index

Prices, 38, 56, 57, 59, 60
Prison, 70, 79, 83, 90, 104, 107, 111, 112
  Wilson in, 84, 85, 88, 89, 91
Private sector, 25, 56, 59, 96
Proceso Intelectual del Uruguay (Zum Felde, 1930), 13–14
Production, 7, 36, 56, 57, 58, 61, 65
Productivity, 33, 58
Profits, 59, 61, 135
Prompt Security Measures (Medidas Prontas de Seguridad), 38, 81
Protectionism, 56, 57, 58, 62, 65, 99, 115, 120, 121, 134
"Protector of Free Peoples" (Artigas), 18
Protests, 68, 71, 82, 84, 140
PST. *See* Partido Socialista de los Trabajadores
Public opinion, 40, 41, 42, 107, 125
Public sector, 23, 25, 30, 31, 33, 36, 56, 62, 101
  budget, 52, 57
  burden on, 35, 59, 138
Punta Carretas Penetentiary, 41
Punta del Este, 2(map), 9, 66, 95
Punta del Este, Camerata, 72
Punta del Este, Charter of (1961), 114

Quijano, Carlos, 106
Quinteros, Elena, 106

Radical Civic Union party (Argentina), 82
Radio, 5, 28, 29, 81, 110
Railroad strike, 103
Railways, 2(map)
Rama, Angel, 14
Rama, Germán, 26
Rancheríos, 9
Ranchers, 16, 28, 42
Ranches, 6, 7, 8
Rapela, Julio C., 78, 81
Real de Azúa, Carlos, 29
Real estate industry, 59, 63, 66
Recargos (artificial exchange rates). *See* Exchange rates
Recession, 61, 62, 63, 65, 66, 67
Records (destruction of), 107–108
Red Cross, 117
Redemocratization, 125, 126, 138
Redistribution, 11, 26, 36
Reflexiones del Batllismo (magazine), 100
Reform, 25, 26. *See also under* Batlle y Ordóñez; Constitution; Elections; Land
Reintegros (tax credits), 58
Religion, 27, 28, 54, 78. *See also* Catholic church
Rent regulation, 66
Repatriation, 61, 97
Representation, 20, 21, 30
República Oriental del Uruguay, 18
Research, 61, 67, 68, 69–70, 71, 95

Resort industry, 9. *See also* Punta del Este
Retirement system, 35, 37
Rhodes, William, 95
Rial, Juan, 49, 84, 86
Rice, 8, 9, 119(table), 123
Río de la Plata. *See* Plata, Río de la
Río Grande do Sul (Brazil), 1
Río Negro (department), 2(map), 9
Rio Treaty, 114, 117
Riqueza y Pobreza del Uruguay: Estudio de las Causas que Retardan el Progreso Nacional (Wealth and Poverty in Uruguay: A Study of the Causes That Retard National Progress) (Martínez Lamas), 10, 11
Rivera, Feliciano, 27–28
Rivera (department), 8
River Plate. *See* Plata, Río de la
Roballa, Alba, 42, 131
Rocha (department), 2(map), 8, 89
Rodó, José Enrique (1872–1917), 14, 83
Rodríguez Camusso, Francisco, 42
Rogríguez Larreta, Eduardo, 140
Rodríguez Monegal, Emir, 14
Rosencof, Mauricio, 14
Roxlo, Carlos, 13
Rouquié, Alain, 129
Rural areas, 4, 5, 9, 11, 26, 27, 29
Ruralismo. *See* Liga Federal de Acción Ruralista
Ruralista movement. *See* Liga Federal de Acción Ruralista

Saenz de Zumarán, Alberto, 85, 88, 90, 92
Saladeros (meat-salting plants), 7
Salida (exit), 80
Salida heróica, 84
Salto (city), 2(map), 5
Salto (department), 2(map)
Sanchez, Florencio, 14
Sanguinetti, Julio María, 90, 94(photo)
  administration, 86, 89, 90, 93, 98, 99, 102, 118, 120–122, 123, 127, 134, 138–139, 142
  candidacy of, 77, 80, 85, 88, 92
  economic policy, 13, 118, 134
  foreign policy, 116, 120–122, 123
  human rights, 105, 106, 108, 127, 128, 140
  prospects, 129, 131, 132
Sangurgo, Francisco, 45
San José (department), 2(map), 9
San Martín, Juan Zorilla de (1888–1931), 14
San Miguel, Fort-Museum of, 17(photo)
Saravia, Aparicio, 19
Sarney, José (Brazil), 123
Schmitter, Philippe, 140
School of the Humanities and Social Sciences, 71
Schools, 11, 27, 69. *See also* Education
Secularization, 3, 27, 29